The Colourful Kitchen Collection

RECIPES FOR HEALTH AND WELLBEING FROM
THE INSTITUTE FOR OPTIMUM NUTRITION

Dedicated to our incredible students and graduates.
Thank you for all you do to help build a healthier future.

First published in 2024 by the Institute for Optimum Nutrition
Ambassador House, Paradise Road, Richmond, TW9 1SQ
www.ion.ac.uk

A record of this book is available from the British Library.

ISBN 978-1-0686413-0-5

Editor and project manager: Catherine Morgan
Deputy editor and project assistant: Hatty Willmoth
Photography: Joy Skipper
Lead designer: Daniela Pop
Assistant designer: Salman Anjum
Cover design: Salman Anjum
Marketing: Carolina Geana and Anne Daly
Proofing: Louise Wates
Index: Brodie Asker
Printing: Contract Publishing UK (CPUK) Limited

"The recipes in The Colourful Kitchen Collection are not only nutritionally sound because they are expertly crafted by ION graduates and the most respected nutrition professionals in the country, they are all utterly delicious too. When you can combine sound nutritional science with culinary magic, indulgence and the pleasure of eating, then you have the most pleasurable way imaginable to care for your long-term wellbeing and take daily steps towards better health."

Dale Pinnock
Clinical nutritionist and chef

"As a nutritionist and lifestyle medicine professional, I find this cookbook a remarkable blend of practical advice, scientific insight and culinary creativity. It's more than just a collection of recipes — it's a well-rounded guide to understanding the intricate relationship between soil fertility, nutrient density and overall human health.

"This cookbook is a must-have for anyone interested in a holistic approach to nutrition. Its inclusive nature, scientific insights and practical recipes make it a valuable resource for nutrition professionals and anyone on a journey toward better health."

British Society of Lifestyle Medicine (BSLM) review panel

"A beautiful culinary road map to eating a 'rainbow diet'! For years, I've been talking about why it's important to eat all the colours found in nature, and this delightful book tells you how to do it in a way that is artful, soulful and full of flavour. A must for every kitchen!"

Deanna Minich, PhD
Author of *The Rainbow Diet*

"Delicious and mouthwatering! This is not just a cookbook with colourful, nutrient-dense recipes but an information source about why soil fertility matters, where to get different phytochemicals and what the benefits are of a rainbow diet. The little snippets about fermented foods, gluten-free, dairy-free or vegan options, and much more allow each home cook to personalise their plate for their needs, supporting the ethos of personalised healthcare we believe in at BANT. Let's get cooking!"

Satu Jackson
CEO of the British Association for Nutrition and Lifestyle Medicine (BANT)

"An all-encompassing cookbook of real food, The Colourful Kitchen Collection is a must have for everyone looking for delicious recipes that help your health."

Sam Feltham
Director of Public Health Collaboration

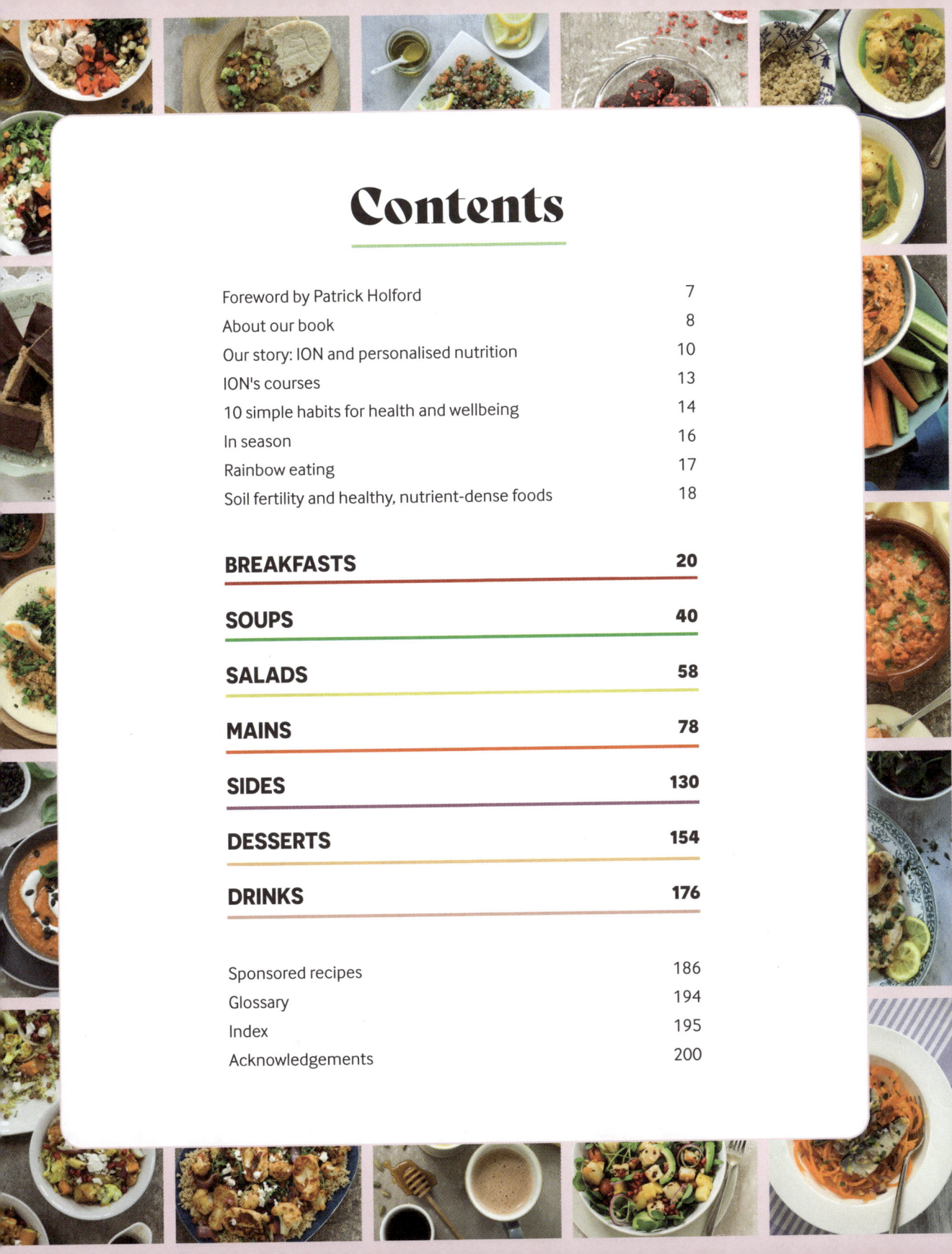

Contents

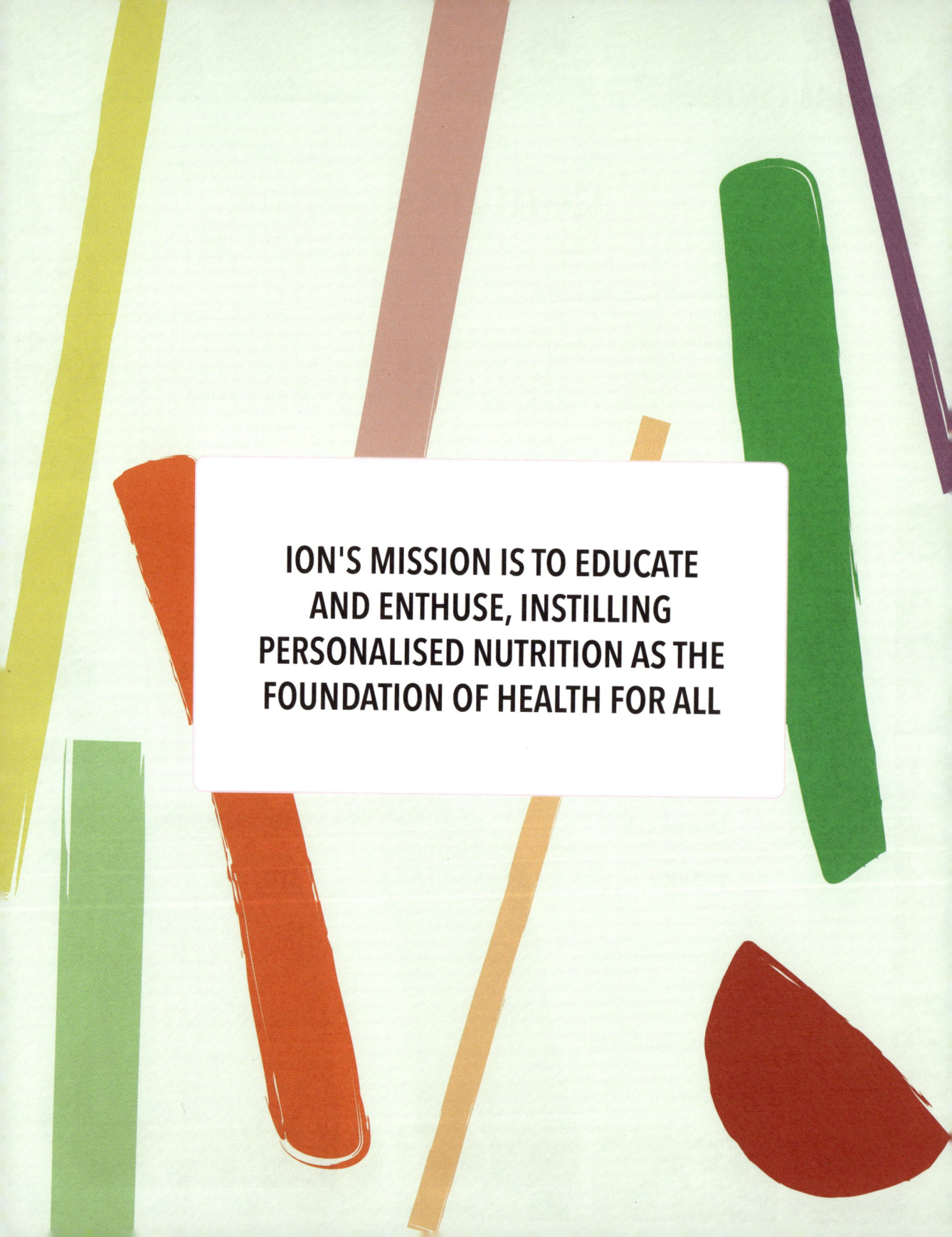

ION'S MISSION IS TO EDUCATE
AND ENTHUSE, INSTILLING
PERSONALISED NUTRITION AS THE
FOUNDATION OF HEALTH FOR ALL

FOREWORD

Forty years ago, 'gluten-free', 'dairy-free', 'essential fat', 'antioxidant' and 'microbiome' didn't exist as expressions in the public domain. That is when the Institute for Optimum Nutrition (ION) came into existence. This cookbook bears testimony to the tremendous increase in nutritional awareness that has taken place since that time. An army of nutritional therapists have not only helped to change the paradigm, but also to make healthy food appealing, desirable and delicious.

The Colourful Kitchen Collection, full of recipes crafted by nutritional therapists and graduates from ION, delivers nuggets of nutritional excellence in the form of food, as well as nutritional wisdom scattered throughout — putting the principles of optimum nutrition into practice. In the same way that there are cultures of cuisine in different countries, *The Colourful Kitchen Collection* adds to the emerging culture of healthy eating, free from ultra-processed foods, low in sugars and high in nutrients including colourful antioxidants, essential fats and fibre.

As ION's founder, back in 1984, when no-one knew about such things as essential fats and antioxidants, and even the concept of 'microbiome' didn't exist, it gives me great pleasure to see the optimum nutrition community grow, share and enjoy delicious food, eaten with the awareness that 'you are what you eat'. This book will be a great resource for years to come for those in the front line of the growing nutrition revolution.

Patrick Holford
Founder Patron of ION

Patrick is a leading spokesman on nutrition and mental health and founder of both the Food for the Brain Foundation and the Institute for Optimum Nutrition (ION).

See page 105 for Patrick's low-carb kedgeree recipe.

🌐 www.patrickholford.com
f patrickholford 📷 @patrickholford.uk

ABOUT OUR BOOK

Welcome to *The Colourful Kitchen Collection: Recipes for Health and Wellbeing from the Institute for Optimum Nutrition* (ION). In this book, you will find 80 recipes from people who studied nutrition with ION, as well as five bonus recipes from our generous sponsors.

These are some of our alumni's favourite recipes for health and wellbeing; food they recommend to their clients and enjoy in their own homes. With each recipe, we've included some information about each contributor and their explanation of why they love the dish so much.

Each recipe in this book has been tested and carefully edited by Catherine Morgan and Hatty Willmoth, and photographed by ION alumna Joy Skipper. Design is by Daniela Pop and Salman Anjum.

The Colourful Kitchen Collection is not a diet book. No diet suits everybody, which is why ION promotes the idea of personalised nutrition (see pages 10-11).

Accordingly, this book contains recipes to support a variety of diets and lifestyles. There are high-fat, low-carb recipes for people on a ketogenic diet. There are higher-carb recipes for those looking for a sweet treat or to refuel after a workout. There are also meaty feasts, plant-based plates and everything in between.

Where possible, we've tried to make it easy to quickly identify which recipes will suit your dietary needs, using icons to indicate allergens as well as whether a recipe is suitable for meat eaters, pescatarians, vegetarians or vegans. However, if you are catering for a food allergy or intolerance, do read product labels carefully — some items can be unexpected sources of allergens (for example, some sauces, dressings and stocks may contain gluten).

Where possible, we want you to be able to tweak, adapt and tailor these recipes to suit you, your body and your kitchen. That's why many of the recipes in this collection include options that enable more people to enjoy them.

The icons represent the recipes, not the serving suggestions. Where multiple icons could be used, we've used the one that includes the most people. For instance, if a recipe can be made with meat or plants, we've labelled

DIETARY NEEDS & ALLERGENS

Recipe contains nuts, dairy or gluten

Recipe doesn't contain nuts, dairy or gluten

Recipe can be made with or without nuts, dairy or gluten

Recipe suitable for meat eaters, pescatarians, vegetarians or vegans

Recipe has a pescetarian, vegetarian or vegan option

it as having a vegan option.

Next to the icons, we've noted the servings and timings of each recipe, and there is a plant count too. Some experts suggest we should be eating at least 30 different plants per week to support the diversity of our gut microbiome, and the plant count makes this easy.

Not only does eating a variety of plant foods help support our gut health, but eating the rainbow, i.e. plant foods in the full spectrum of colours, is a good way to eat most of the nutrients our bodies need without thinking about them.

That's why some of the ingredient lists in this book are quite long. It's also why this book is called *The Colourful Kitchen Collection* — we weren't fibbing!

That's not to say all these recipes are super complicated. We do have a few culinary challenges in here, and some that take a while to make – but there are plenty of quick, simple recipes too.

Plus, every dish should be achievable in a kitchen without lots of fancy appliances. Where air fryers and spiralisers have been used, we've given alternatives, so that no-one's left out.

There are some unusual ingredients, so we've suggested swaps that are cheaper or easier to find wherever possible. We've also removed where our contributors have specified an ingredient should be organic. Organic food is unaffordable to some, and a must for others; we've left that choice to you.

The Colourful Kitchen Collection is split into the following sections: breakfasts, soups, salads, mains, sides, desserts, drinks and sponsors' recipes.

BREAKFASTS

SOUPS

SALADS

MAINS

SIDES

DESSERTS

DRINKS

SPONSORS

There is no section for snacks. Studies are mixed on the health effects of snacking, so if you are someone for whom healthy snacking works well, there are plenty of snackable dishes in this book, especially the sides and desserts.

That's right – we have a dessert section. Sweet treats may not be a stereotypical health food, and they may not be appropriate for those on low-sugar or low-carb diets.

However, for those who do have a sweet tooth, it might be helpful to know of some nutritious options.

Some of the desserts in this book are relatively low in sugar, and many are completely free from refined sugars, so they tend to taste rich but not very sweet. You'll find lots of dates and fresh fruit, as well as coconut oil, seeds, nuts and nut butters, which help these dishes have a slower effect on blood sugars and feel more filling than some traditional desserts.

Breakfast might not be something you eat. Many intermittent fasters choose to elongate their overnight fasts by skipping breakfast or eating later in the morning. Meanwhile, others reject the idea that breakfast food should be its own unique category.

Many people in the UK are stuck in a cereal-and-milk routine, which is why our breakfasts section contains a spectrum of dishes – from granola to burrito bowls – to gently challenge breakfasters to think outside the box, while providing some conventional options. Of course, you can eat this food at any time of day and, if you want to eat soup, salad or stew for breakfast, go for it!

Towards the end of the book, we have a section of recipes provided by our generous sponsors who have made this book possible, and to whom we are so grateful. Thank you!

Thank you, too, to our wonderful graduates who submitted their recipes to be included in this book. We've loved working with you – and your food is delicious.

And thank you to you for buying this book and embarking on your journey towards optimum nutrition. We hope you love these recipes as much as we do.

Love,

The ION Cookbook Team

OUR STORY: ION AND PERSONALISED NUTRITION

The Institute for Optimum Nutrition (ION) is a higher education charity that offers training to those who are new to nutrition, to qualified nutritional therapy practitioners and to allied healthcare professionals looking to expand their practice. We are proud to be one of the first providers of nutritional therapy training in the UK, and remain committed to providing courses delivered by an experienced, highly-qualified faculty of academics and clinical and research supervisors.

Through all our activities, we promote the principles of optimum nutrition as complementary practice to medicine. We do this through our:

- Nutritional therapy training courses: BSc (Hons) Nutritional Therapy and Graduate Diploma in Integrative Functional Nutrition
- Professional Dietary Educator course: CertHE Personalised Diet and Health
- Short courses for professionals (e.g. doctors, allied healthcare practitioners and CAM practitioners)
- Accredited professional CPD courses
- Informative content hub and outreach activities

Our vision is for optimum nutrition for all, throughout life, and our mission is to educate and enthuse, instilling personalised nutrition as the foundation of health for all.

The Institute for Optimum Nutrition (ION) was established in 1984 following two realisations made by our founder Patrick Holford. Working with our late Patron, twice Nobel Laureate Dr Linus Pauling, Patrick realised that many modern western diseases were the direct consequence of sub-optimal nutrition. Yet they could be prevented and, in some cases, reversed by 'nutritional medicine'.

Linus Pauling called this 'orthomolecular medicine'; we called it 'optimum nutrition'.

Based on a naturopathic philosophy, optimum nutrition sets out that the optimal intake of a nutrient is what is required to restore or ensure health. Linus Pauling predicted that it would be "the medicine of tomorrow".

The second realisation Patrick had was that putting optimum nutrition into practice would require a new profession of nutritional therapists. These highly-trained professionals could work directly with people, or in collaboration with doctors; identifying and advising when higher amounts of nutrients were needed to restore biochemical balance, or on appropriate lifestyle changes such as movement and stress reduction. To answer this challenge, Patrick founded the Institute for Optimum Nutrition, which has been actively engaged in training ever since.

Since ION's founding, evidence has continued to show that optimal amounts of specific nutrients may improve immunity against infection, and help to prevent, halt the progression of, and in some cases even reverse conditions such as type 2 diabetes, cardiovascular disease, depression, dementia and other mental illnesses.

Yet one size does not fit all. Our responses to food after eating vary widely and we all have different dietary preferences, health goals, health journeys and genetic makeup. It is this concept of individuality that forms the foundation of personalised nutrition. For a nutritional therapy practitioner, these unique requirements help inform recommendations to guide clients towards making effective and lasting dietary and lifestyle changes – that work for them. For the client, this personalised approach to healthcare can be empowering, and enables them to take a more active role in their health and wellbeing.

As a core component of the functional medicine model, which looks beyond symptoms to identify and address the root causes of illness, personalised nutrition puts the person – not the disease – at the centre, and views the human body as more than the sum of its parts. Practitioners strive to identify underlying imbalances within the body (e.g. in biological systems, the microbiome, nutrient status, etc.), and to correct them using real, whole foods, as well as lifestyle interventions and supplements where appropriate. This practice of using nutrition to support health is also referred to as 'functional nutrition'.

Practitioners skilled in the personalised nutrition approach will analyse a client's health and family history, diet, lifestyle and environment to identify potential factors contributing to ill or sub-optimal health. Functional tests may also inform recommendations based on each person's unique biology, such as genetic predispositions to nutrient deficiencies, food allergies, hormone imbalances and toxic exposures. Advice will then be personalised to suit their individual requirements.

Although registered nutritional therapists cannot diagnose or treat disease, they can work in preventative healthcare and support those with existing conditions using personalised nutrition. This includes working to support clients with chronic health issues such as diabetes, obesity or cardiovascular disease; anyone with persistent digestive issues or an autoimmune condition; or more simply anyone looking to enhance their health and wellbeing – be it increasing their energy levels, supporting digestion or optimising their training fitness.

Heather Rosa, Dean at the Institute for Optimum Nutrition, says:

"Nutritional therapists don't just work with people who are very unwell. We work with people who want to stay well. For instance, if you want to prevent or delay a condition because it's in the family or you're someone who just wants to improve their fitness, a session with a nutritional therapist could be a good place to start.

"With increasing demands being placed on the health service, the answer has to be in prevention if we really hope to reduce the burden on the already overburdened NHS. We also need to empower people so that they know they have the means to affect their own health and wellbeing journey where it relates to diet and lifestyle choices.

"When people know that small changes can have a positive and lasting impact, it empowers them to take back control of their health – and this is the message that we want to get across to people."

"I thoroughly enjoyed the Graduate Diploma... The supportive nature of the teachers made the challenging course content manageable. The online course structure was perfect for me, living in Spain while running a practice and being a full-time mom!

"I chose ION because, as a functional nurse practitioner, I felt like I needed additional nutritional training and was thrilled with the functional nutrition and behaviour change focuses of the programme. I am grateful to all the professors and my class community!"

Kaley Johnson (GDip graduate)

"I've always wanted to help people with autoimmune diseases, especially those facing symptoms similar to mine. Completing the course at ION opened my eyes to how nutrition and lifestyle changes can transform autoimmune health. It also gave me the tools to apply my scientific knowledge in practice. It may sound cliché, but watching my clients improve and feel better about themselves is the most rewarding part."

Victoria (VJ) Hamilton (DipION graduate)

"As part of the first cohort of the part-time degree course at ION, I've thoroughly enjoyed the journey. The range of modules and the diverse expertise of the lecturers have kept the course engaging, which is essential for the 4.5-year course.

"The in-depth, up to date curriculum covers all aspects of nutritional therapy, providing a solid foundation in both theory and practice. It has equipped me with the comprehensive knowledge and skills I need to confidently pursue a career as a nutritional therapist."

Helen Hindley (BSc student)

"I'm grateful to have studied at ION due to their brilliant lecturers and their scientific, evidence-based approach to nutritional therapy, which has provided an excellent foundation for my career as a women's health nutritionist."

Shaz Sarchamy (DipION graduate)

"The course has given me so much more than I expected. The practice management module was invaluable in getting me off on the right track in starting my business. I now have my own business specialising in autoimmune conditions which I love. It allows me to be completely myself and to spend my time and energy on the things that matter to me in life."

Kate Potter (DipION graduate)

"The skills I gained [studying at ION] make me feel like a much more rounded nutritional therapist and give me confidence in my ability to help my clients using the latest evidence. The learnings from the research project have fundamentally changed how I read and apply nutrition research and therefore how I advise my clients."

Nicky Clark (BSc Top-up graduate)

"Graduating from ION has been one of the most important moments in my life. I was finally able to begin living my dream to become a health practitioner and writer. Working with my clients and seeing them reverse symptoms that they have dealt with for a long time is heartening and inspiring and really makes this job so rewarding.

"I am truly living a life I love. I thank ION for the first-class training and education I received in my nutritional therapy diploma. It really gave me a solid foundation for everything I have been involved in since my graduation."

Virginia Richardson (DipION graduate)

"The Graduate Diploma provided me with an amazing framework to use on how we should see the body as a network of interconnected systems, underpinned by science to develop strategies to support sustainable change and help others on their health journey. It has helped me to adapt my thinking and approach to personalised nutrition and has brought together my many years of science and nutrition experience to give me a practical base which I can adapt to suit clients' individual needs. Thank you ION!"

Debbie Pyke (GDip graduate)

ION'S COURSES

What we do

The Institute for Optimum Nutrition (ION) has a broad range of courses on offer for those who wish to embark on further study, whether entering higher education for the first time, retraining as a nutritional therapist or enriching their career in a complementary profession with nutritional know-how. With extensive experience and a strong university partnership, you know you're in safe hands.

As a charity, we're dedicated to educating the public about nutrition – not just our students – so if you're not looking to study nutrition, you can still learn with us by following us on **social media**, subscribing to our monthly **newsletter**, reading our **articles**, watching our **videos** and listening to our **podcast**.

Getting started

If you just want a little taste of studying nutrition with us, check out our **short course in Diet and Health**. It will give you a thorough grounding in diet and lifestyle approaches to health and wellbeing. Learn to enrich your own health, or your career if you work in a related field.

For a little extra expertise, enrol on the **Cert HE in Personalised Diet and Health**. This is similar to the short course above, but it also provides a solid grounding in health sciences and will enable you to start your career as a diet and lifestyle educator if you so choose. It's ideal for health coaches, personal trainers, complementary therapists, etc. who wish to inform their practices with a nutrition qualification.

Ready to study for a full degree? Consider our **BSc (Hons) Nutritional Therapy**. It combines the latest theoretical and applied knowledge from nutrition, research, science and the psychology of behaviour change with real world clinical training. With this degree, you will qualify as a nutritional therapist and can register with BANT (the professional body).

If you're looking to study on our degree, you'll need to know a bit about the science first. No science background? No problem! Simply take our **Science Access** course to begin your studies.

Already a qualified nutritional therapist?

If you're already a diploma nutritional therapist but want a degree with us, our **BSc (Hons) Nutritional Therapy Top-up** course is a fast way to do just that.

And if you're a qualified nutritional therapist who has been out of practice for three years or more, you can renew your career and credentials with our **Return to Practice**.

If you just want to stay up to date with your nutrition knowledge, join us for our online **Continuing Professional Development** courses and workshops.

Want to integrate nutrition into current practice?

Are you a doctor, pharmacist, dentist, nurse or allied healthcare practitioner looking to study nutrition? Our **Graduate Diploma Integrative Functional Nutrition** is for you. It's designed for those working in healthcare settings to integrate the principles of personalised nutrition into their practice.

If you also take our **Clinical Practice module**, you can work as a nutritional therapist under BANT and the CNHC (the regulator) after graduating with our Graduate Diploma.

Looking for a bitesize approach?

If you can't commit to studying a full Graduate Diploma with us right now, start by taking some of its modules as **credit bearing short courses**. Learn at your own pace and accumulate credits towards a Graduate Diploma. Alternatively, choose non-credit bearing versions to deepen your subject knowledge without assessment.

Find out more

Check out our website at **www.ion.ac.uk** or call us on (+44) 020 8614 7800

10 SIMPLE HABITS FOR HEALTH AND WELLBEING

Diet plays a fundamental role in health and disease but is just one part of the wellness picture. Whilst food is the foundation of any nutrition and lifestyle programme, there are additional pillars of health that contribute to our physical and mental wellbeing, including relationships, relaxation, sleep and movement. So, whilst our bodies are fuelled by food, they are also nurtured by the way we live.

When it comes to improving our health, small changes can make a big difference — and they don't have to be costly or radical. Here are 10 simple habits to support body and mind.

Eat mindfully

Common habits such as eating on the go, eating on autopilot and rushing meals, can hinder the digestive process and lead to overeating and poor food choices. Eating mindfully simply means being present with our food and the eating experience.

TIP
Aim for distraction-free mealtimes — that means no screens at the dinner table. Slow the pace, chew well and really notice the food, including its aroma, flavour and texture.

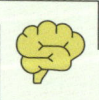

Switch off

Our minds need time to rest, which means taking some time off from the constant stimulation, blue light exposure and never-ending negative news cycles that fill our screens and feeds. Although it can be difficult to fully disconnect, there are benefits to switching off from external noise and negativity from time to time.

TIP
Break the habit of mindlessly 'doomscrolling' through negative news stories and social media posts, and try to find some space to be quiet and still.

Rest the digestive system

It's not just about what we eat, but also when we eat and how often. Intermittent fasting-type eating patterns or simply spacing out meals can give the digestive system a well-earned break, and may bring other health benefits too.

TIP
Changes don't need to be extreme. It could be as simple as leaving a few hours between meals without snacking or lengthening a night-time break with an earlier dinner or later breakfast. A word of caution: this may not be suitable for everyone (e.g. during pregnancy, if underweight or at risk of an eating disorder, or if there's an underlying health issue), so seek professional advice if necessary.

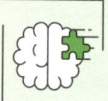

Nurture a positive mindset

Directing attention and energy towards the positives in life, no matter how small, can help crowd out negative thoughts, improve mental and emotional wellbeing, and flip from glass half empty to glass half full thinking.

TIP
Spend 10 minutes at the beginning or end of each day to reflect on the things that have gone well and appreciate any positive moments. Keep a journal if you prefer to write things down.

Move

Incorporating movement and exercise into our daily routines can help us live healthier and happier lives. It doesn't have to be strenuous, either — walking, yoga, cycling, rebounding and active play can all have beneficial effects on body and mind.

TIP
Get moving! Find an activity that's enjoyable, join a group for extra support, step away from the desk/sofa to get some movement in, swap the lift for the stairs... Breaking exercise into smaller chunks (aka 'exercise snacks') throughout the day can be effective and more manageable.

Choose real, whole foods

There may be differing views within the nutrition community regarding best dietary practices (plant-based vs. vegan vs. carnivore vs. ketogenic, and so on), but there is also common ground: a healthy diet should prioritise nutrient-dense, whole foods and minimise food that is ultra-processed, nutrient-poor, and high in refined sugar and industrially processed cooking oils and spreads.

TIP Identify and address your healthy eating barriers. If it's lack of time or cost, for example, simple strategies such as meal planning or batch cooking can help. Also, focus on adding foods into the diet rather than taking them away.

Focus on sleep

Good quality, restorative sleep is vital for optimising health. While the odd bad night's sleep is unlikely to cause long-term harm, regular or prolonged periods of poor shut-eye will eventually take its toll — physically, mentally and emotionally.

TIP Prioritise sleep! Establish a healthy routine so the body knows it's time to rest, and avoid screens, sugar, caffeine and other stimulants before bedtime. If racing or anxious thoughts are impacting sleep, find ways to relax — a warm bath, music, meditation, deep-breathing, or anything that helps calm the mind. A comfortable environment is important too.

Strengthen connections

Life can be tough without support. Being part of a community and fostering connections with those around us can help give our lives meaning, increase happiness and reduce stress and isolation.

TIP Reconnect with friends and family, join a local hobby group or volunteer for a favourite cause, and make the time to have conversations and develop positive relationships.

Find purpose

Having a sense of purpose could help us live longer, healthier and more fulfilling lives. A strong sense of purpose may help support mental and physical health, social connections, and resilience — and is one commonality observed among elders living in so-called Blue Zones.

TIP Self-reflection is key. What are you good at? What do you care about? How can you use your skills to help others? Find a reason to get up each morning and make life meaningful.

Manage stress

Stress is a normal physiological response to a potentially threatening situation — and is useful under certain circumstances. However, stress that is extreme, repeated or prolonged can be detrimental to our physical, mental and emotional wellbeing, and has been associated with numerous health problems.

TIP Whilst stress is an inevitable part of life, it's possible to manage our exposure and response to it — for example: by having a strong support system (family, friends, community, etc.); learning to say no; switching off negativity; and practising stress-reduction techniques such as meditation, breathwork, yoga or any hobby or activity that helps calm the mind.

IN SEASON

It can be difficult to eat seasonally when you cook from recipes. If a dish specifies asparagus, it requires asparagus, regardless of whether they're in season. Of course, asparagus will be in season somewhere in the world – just perhaps not in your local area.

Seasonal eating refers to a pattern of consumption that follows the local seasons, buying food that hasn't had to travel far to reach your plate. It usually refers to fresh plant produce, i.e. fruit and vegetables, but some animal products have their optimal seasons too.

Choosing your food according to when it is in season locally has so many benefits. For a start, it's likely to be better for the environment. Local produce doesn't need to be transported long distances, so it tends to have a lower carbon footprint.

The perks translate to financial savings too; in-season, locally grown food tends to be cheaper, because there are fewer costs associated with farming, storage and transportation.

It is also likely to be fresher. Fruit and vegetables that travel long distances are often picked way before they are ripe so they don't spoil by the time they reach the shop shelf, whereas local food can be picked ripe and sold fresh.

This means in-season produce is not only more delicious, but more nutritious. Food that's left on the plant until it's ripe tends to contain more vitamins, minerals and antioxidants than food picked early, as it has had longer to benefit from the soil's goodness. Plus, once a fruit or vegetable is picked, its nutritional value begins depleting – in some cases, quite dramatically – so the quicker the journey from earth to mouth, the better.

So, fresh, ripe, local produce is generally best for the environment, your wallet, your taste buds and your health. But how do we start eating with the seasons?

If you buy your fruit and vegetables from supermarkets, as most of us do, seasonal eating means checking food labels and trying to buy British produce. If this is your strategy, it helps to know roughly when foods are going in and out of season, so you don't have to check every label.

Freezing food helps preserve its nutritional value – and even enhance it, in some cases. So, buying frozen food, or buying in-season veggies to freeze and eat throughout the year, are both good options.

Alternatively, think outside the supermarket box. Buying your fruit and vegetables from farmers' markets or veg box delivery services ensures your fresh food is local and in season, without having to do much mental work.

Even better, grow food yourself – in a garden, an allotment or plant pots – or go foraging, as long as you're confident you can do this safely, e.g. with a foraging club.

Buying food in season means limiting your choices, and that can be frustrating when trying to cook from recipes that require specific ingredients. But we encourage you to be flexible and creative with the ingredients suggested in this book, to fit what's available in your area. For example, asparagus is only in season in spring, so at other times of year, swap it with tenderstem broccoli or green beans.

This chart might come in handy if you get stuck.

SPRING — Artichokes, Asparagus, Beetroots, Carrots, Lettuce, Peas, Radishes, Rocket, Spinach, Spring onions, Apricots, Blueberries, Cherries, Lemons, Limes, Rhubarb, Strawberries

SUMMER — Aubergines, Broccoli, Courgettes, Cucumber, Fennel, New potatoes, Peppers, Sweetcorn, Turnips, Mangetout, Melons, Plums, Nectarines, Peaches, Pears

AUTUMN — Kale, Leeks, Marrows, Mushrooms, Parsnips, Potatoes, Pumpkins, Shallots, Sweet potatoes, Figs, Apples, Bananas, Clementines, Grapefruit

WINTER — Brussels sprouts, Butternut squash, German turnip, Cauliflower, Artichokes, Blood oranges, Cranberries, Dates, Kiwi, Pomegranate

RAINBOW EATING

The images in this book wouldn't look so appealing if they were all beige. Their vibrancy makes them seem all the more delicious — and eating a colourful diet may also bring health benefits.

'The rainbow diet' and 'rainbow eating' refer to a pattern of eating through which an individual aims to eat all the colours of the rainbow. This means plenty of plants: red tomatoes, orange butternut squash, yellow corn, green broccoli, blueberries, purple carrots and bright pink beetroot. The rainbow diet also includes a 'white or brown' category — despite not appearing on actual rainbows!

The whole point of 'eating the rainbow' is that it's an easy way to eat lots of different types of plant foods that contain different beneficial nutrients, to get in as much nutritional good stuff as possible. We need vitamins and minerals to support good health, but they're present in different plants in different amounts, so eating a wide variety of plants helps us get a bit of everything.

It's not just the big names like vitamin C that a rainbow diet pulls in, either. It's also all the little phytochemicals — compounds derived from plants — that most of us may have never even heard of, and which potentially come with a multitude of benefits.

Many of these phytochemicals play a part in a plant's colour, so the hues on our plate can give us some indication about the diversity of phytochemicals we might be feeding our bodies.

This is all relatively under-researched so we can't be sure that rainbow eating itself is uniquely beneficial. Also, there are some people for whom a rainbow diet would not be best; for example, people with intolerances to plant compounds such as lectins, or following a meat-focused ketogenic diet may struggle to eat the rainbow without compromising an eating pattern that works for them.

For many of us, however, aiming to eat colourfully is a low-risk, healthful eating strategy to maximise our nutrition without having to think too much. Plus, it's beautiful! Eating is a multi-sensory experience, and we're more likely to want to eat, and enjoy eating, a colourful plate of food.

Rainbow eating also helps the majority of guts benefit from a variety of different plant fibres, by cultivating a diverse and thriving community of gut microbes, which in turn supports whole-body health.

It's one reason that this is *The Colourful Kitchen Collection*. What's not to love?

PURPLE ——————————— ANTHOCYANINS
Blackberries, Blueberries, Blackcurrants, Red cabbage, Plums, Radicchio, Red onions, Red grapes, Aubergines

PINK & RED ——————————— LYCOPENE / VITAMIN C
Tomatoes, Watermelon, Grapefruit, Red bell peppers, Pomegranate, Cherries, Strawberries, Rhubarb, Beetroot

ORANGE & YELLOW ————— CAROTENOIDS, E.G. BETA–CAROTENE / LUTEIN
Carrots, Butternut squash, Pumpkin, Corn, Papaya, Sweet potato, Oranges, Nectarines, Apricots, Lemons

WHITE & BROWN ————— ALLICIN / FLAVONOIDS / POTASSIUM
Mushrooms, Garlic, Cauliflower, White onions, Parsnips, Potatoes, Daikon radish, Chickpeas, Turnips

GREEN ——————— INDOLES / CAROTENOIDS / SAPONINS / FOLATE
Broccoli, Spinach, Asparagus, Kale, Avocado, Pears, Courgette, White grapes, Kiwi, Spring greens, Cabbage

SOIL FERTILITY AND HEALTHY, NUTRIENT-DENSE FOODS

By Dian Shepperson Mills

Dian's research interests are endometriosis, sub-fertility, endocrine disorders, coeliac disease and the gut microbiome, She has been a Trustee of the Endometriosis SHE Trust UK charity, attending world conferences, and is a Trustee of the Institute for Optimum Nutrition (ION).

Dian is the Director of The Endometriosis and Fertility Clinic and a certified nutritional therapist, helping many women regain their health. She is also a member of the American Society of Reproductive Medicine.

⊕ www.endometriosis.co.uk
⊕ www.makingbabies.com

Humankind requires healthy food to survive and thrive. Clean air and rainwater falling on the crops build nutrient-rich soils, the sunshine enriches the earth and engenders photosynthesis. Growing healthy plants is crucial for the health of every generation. We can see its importance in the Blue Zone countries, where people are living long, healthy lives, eating fresh foods.

Soil is alive, full of chemicals and biological matter that are essential to improve our health. When farmers, home gardeners and allotment holders tend the soil well, they create a nutrient-rich environment for plants, which then grow and feed us. When plant crops and trees die, the basic material goes back into the soil to be reused.

The health of a nation depends upon its soil quality, but in the UK, the nutrients in the soil are depleted. It is suffering the effects of long-term use of pesticides, fungicides and artificial fertilisers that have damaged the natural soil biome.

Healthy soil is important for the growth of microbes and plant roots. Soil is a mixture of sand, silt and loams – it needs to hold moisture and be able to drain appropriately. We know that the capacity of soil to hold and drain water depends on the organic matter it contains. When cover crops like cowpeas, sweet clover and sorghum punch their roots deep into the soil, they open channels for crops to reach water and nutrients, supporting the growth and health of plants.

Topsoil should be rich and nutrient laden. Nutrients pass from the soil to the plant's roots, so the absence of a single trace element in the soil can result in that same absence in food, which can in turn harm our health. For instance, if the mineral cobalt is missing from the soil and thus our food, we may struggle to produce vitamin B12 in our bodies. When people become deficient in vitamin B12, they are unable to use iron properly, and may become anaemic and vulnerable to disease. The presence of cobalt within vitamin B12 governs our ability to uptake eight other elements: vanadium, chromium, manganese, iron, nickel, copper, zinc and molybdenum. Other elements, such as calcium, magnesium and potash, help plants to resist disease and extend their shelf life. Our health and food security depends on this knowledge.

Each teaspoonful of fertile soil from the biofilm surrounding crop root hairs is teaming with 600 million bacteria. These bacteria decompose the organic matter, converting nutrients into their own body biomass that plants can use as food. The bacteria are aided by their predators: the protozoa, nematodes, microarthropods, and earthworms. In turn, they are prey for all the millipedes, centipedes, beetles, etc. Soil fungi help to decompose organic matter, mineralising and delivering nutrients into the roots – the food chain.

But this has been disrupted by modern agriculture. Farming became formulaic in the '60s, '70s, '80s and '90s, using chemical fertilisers for crops and synthetic inputs to improve yields, creating toxic side-effects in the environment that still affect public health today, throwing the entire soil ecosystem out of balance. We need to keep the soils viable; our lifelong health depends upon soil health. The farmers desperately need our support to return the tired, depleted soils to their former glory. But we can enhance soil quality with the help of the government and organisations such as the Soil Association.

The Soil Association has devised a seven-point plan to guide British farmers, allotment keepers, gardeners and smallholders on how they can restore and increase nutrient density and vibrancy in the 747 types of soil on these islands. This is that plan:

1. Monitor soil health
2. Increase the amount of plant and animal matter going back into the land
3. Improve soil life by reducing tillage and chemicals
4. Cover up bare soil with continuous plant cover
5. Bring more trees onto farmland
6. Reduce soil compaction from heavy machinery and livestock
7. Design crop rotations to improve soil health

Farming from healthy soils would ensure that healthier crops could be grown. Let us hope that similar templates for soil fertility are adopted in many countries.

But not all food must come from farmed land. Do you have a window ledge, balcony or maybe a patch of neglected lawn? Why not grow some fruit, vegetables or herbs, and enjoy the delicious flavours bursting forth from your own handiwork? Herbs are good-to-go from pots on a window ledge and are full of beneficial nutrients.

You may branch out as your confidence grows, and perhaps take on a bigger project, such as renting a half-plot allotment. There, you'll become part of a whole community of like-minded people, sharing plants and recipes. The healing fresh air, exercise and natural daylight don't go amiss either, alongside all the healthy fresh produce you'll grow.

There is satisfaction to be had from planting, growing and eating your own homegrown food. Humankind has stressed our blue-green planet, and it is now time to give back. We all need to replenish soils, preserve a healthy way of life, and eat seasonal foods rather than the ultra-processed meals being thrust into public view.

Food is worth far more than gold; it is your lifetime of health. Let's build a healthy nation from the soil up!

Breakfasts

> "If you've not used an air fryer before, think of it as a small but powerful oven. As a nutritional therapist, I feel an air fryer is a fantastic tool to reduce the time it takes to make your own meals from scratch."

AIR FRYER GRANOLA

Jenny says: *"Making your own granola puts you in control of the ingredients. Use this recipe as a guide and make your own bespoke granola quickly and easily using your air fryer."*

SERVES	TIME	PLANTS
4	20 mins	5+

METHOD

1. Put the coconut oil, honey and vanilla extract on a baking dish that fits your air fryer and place in the cold air fryer.
2. Set the air fryer to 160°C and the timer to 15 minutes.
3. In a bowl, mix the oats, nuts, seeds, chia seeds, cinnamon and salt.
4. Add this mixture to the dish in the air fryer once it is up to heat and stir well.
5. Stir regularly as the granola bakes to ensure even cooking.
6. Cook for up to 15 minutes and then leave to cool.
7. Serve once cool.

TO MAKE WITHOUT AN AIR FRYER

1. Preheat the oven to 180°C/160°C fan/gas mark 4 and line a baking tray with parchment paper.
2. In a small pan, heat the coconut oil, honey and vanilla extract on a low heat, stirring.
3. When melted, combine with the dry ingredients in a bowl, mix well and spread out on a baking tray.
4. Cook in the oven for 20 mins or until golden brown, stirring regularly.

INGREDIENTS

- 60g coconut oil
- 60g runny honey
- 1 tsp vanilla extract
- 140g porridge oats
- 65g chopped nuts
- 65g mixed seeds
- 20g chia seeds
- 1 tsp cinnamon
- Pinch of salt

 SWAPS

Vegan: use maple syrup instead of honey
Nut-free: use seeds only; omit the nuts
Gluten-free: use gluten-free oats

RECIPE BY JENNY TSCHIESCHE

Jenny is a *Sunday Times* No.1 bestselling author and has written several cookbooks. In addition to writing books, Jenny also sees clients, delivers workshops, works with schools and athletes, and partners with companies such as supermarkets, all in her capacity as a nutritional therapist.

 www.jennytschiesche.com 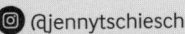 @jennytschiesche

GRAIN-FREE GRANOLA

MAKES	TIME	PLANTS
1 large jar	40 mins	10

INGREDIENTS

- 250g almonds, hazelnuts, walnuts and pecan nuts, roughly chopped
- 100g desiccated or flaked coconut
- 50g pumpkin seeds
- 50g sunflower seeds
- 50g ground flaxseed
- 50g coconut oil
- 100g almond butter
- 1 tsp ground cinnamon
- 1 tsp vanilla extract
- 1 large egg white

Julia says: *"Many shop bought granolas are high in sugar, but this version is sugar-free and rich in protein and healthy fats, so will help keep your blood sugar stable and you full until lunch. It contains pumpkin seeds which are a good source of B vitamins, omega-3 fats and zinc.*

"Enjoy this granola with Greek or natural yoghurt, a dairy-free alternative, or milk of your choice. Add some berries to up your antioxidants; raspberries, blueberries and blackberries go particularly well. The recipe makes a large batch, so you'll get plenty of servings."

METHOD

1. Preheat the oven to 180°C/160°C fan/gas mark 4.
2. Combine all the dry ingredients (except cinnamon) in a large bowl.
3. In a small saucepan, melt the coconut oil and combine with the almond butter, cinnamon and vanilla extract.
4. In a separate bowl, beat the egg white until it forms stiff peaks.
5. Fold the almond butter mixture into the dry ingredients until combined, then fold in the egg white.
6. Spread the mixture evenly over a lined baking tray and bake for 20 minutes, or until golden.
7. Once cool, crumble into clusters. Store in an airtight jar and consume within 1-2 weeks.

⇆ **SWAPS**

Vegan: replace the egg with 1 tbsp chia seeds and 2½ tbsp water

RECIPE BY JULIA YOUNG

Julia is a registered nutritional therapist specialising in fertility. She helps couples struggling to conceive to realise their dream of having a family. Julia offers personalised nutrition and lifestyle support and believes in the importance of getting to the root cause of people's fertility issues.

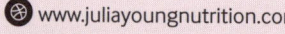 www.juliayoungnutrition.com 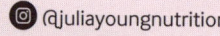 @juliayoungnutrition

IBD-ADAPTABLE CHIA PORRIDGE

Clemmie says: *"Porridge is a firm favourite for breakfast with many of our clients and is a great option to start the day, but often people with IBD fear it when they are in a flare. I love empowering clients with practical tips to adapt recipes like this to ensure they can still enjoy what they love, whether their IBD is in remission, or they're in a flare. This recipe is not only tasty and filling, it provides important energy and soluble fibre from the oats, chia seeds and fruit which can help to reduce both diarrhoea and constipation, common symptoms in IBD."*

SERVES	TIME	PLANTS
1	10 mins	3+

TOPPINGS – choose at least 1 from each column
(adaptations for flare in brackets)

Protein
(important for growth and repair)

- Dairy or soya yoghurt
- Peanut butter *(smooth)*
- Almond butter *(smooth)*
- Almonds *(ground)*
- Walnuts *(ground)*
- Any other nuts or seeds *(ground)*

Flavour
Cinnamon/cocoa/vanilla extract/honey

Fruit
(important source of soluble fibre, nutrients and antioxidants)

- Banana
- Apple *(skinned and stewed)*
- Pear *(skinned and stewed)*
- Strawberries or other berries *(as tolerated – blend, mash or sieve as needed)*

INGREDIENTS

- 40g oats (gluten-free if needed)
- 200ml milk of choice, and extra for desired consistency
- 1 tbsp chia seeds (milled chia in an IBD flare)

TOPPING COMBINATION IDEAS

(adapt texture of ingredients as needed)

- Cocoa, almond butter and banana
- Cinnamon, apple and walnuts
- Peanut butter, banana and honey
- Almonds, vanilla extract and strawberries

METHOD

1. Put the oats and milk into a pan and bring to a steady simmer for around 5 minutes, stirring regularly to make a nice creamy porridge. Towards the end, add the chia seeds and choice of extra flavours and stir in. The porridge will thicken when the chia is added so add more milk or some water to get your desired consistency.
2. Place into a bowl and top with your choice of fruit and nuts/nut butter.

RECIPE BY CLEMMIE OLIVER

Clemmie is a qualified nutritional therapist, registered associate nutritionist and founder of the Nutrition and Lifestyle Medicine Clinic which supports people living with inflammatory bowel diseases (IBD) to improve their quality of life. Clemmie also regularly speaks on the topic of nutrition at companies of all sizes in the UK and globally.

 www.nalmclinic.com @clemmieolivernutrition

GUT-SOOTHING STEWED APPLES

SERVES	TIME	PLANTS
4	10-15 mins	4

INGREDIENTS

- 120ml water
- 4 eating apples (any variety), chopped with skins left on
- 1 star anise
- 1 tsp cinnamon
- 2 cloves

Amie says: *"This is such a simple recipe that I often recommend to clients as it can be eaten for breakfast or dessert. Stewed apples contain a soluble fibre called pectin, which has been found to support the mucosal layer of the intestine. Apple skin is also full of minerals, fibre and a special plant compound called quercetin that may have anti-inflammatory effects."*

METHOD

1. Pour the water into a saucepan and add the chopped apple and spices.
2. Bring to a boil and then simmer for about 10-15 minutes, until the apples are soft. Keep stirring and don't let the pan dry out.
3. Leave to cool before serving.

Serving suggestion: serve with Greek yoghurt or coconut yoghurt, add to porridge, or eat it on its own. A drizzle of maple syrup can be added for sweetness, if desired.

RECIPE BY AMIE BUTLER

Amie is a passionate registered nutritional therapist based in Whitstable, Kent. She completed her studies at the Institute for Optimum Nutrition (ION) in 2019. With a keen focus on gut health and weight management, Amie champions a 'food-first' philosophy, crafting personalised nutrition plans that cater to each client's unique needs. Her practice epitomises an individual-centered approach to healthcare, ensuring every client receives tailored and evidence-informed guidance.

 www.amiebutlernutrition.co.uk   @amiebutlernutrition

" Opt for different apple varieties as these offer unique combinations of vitamins, minerals and antioxidants. "

> This recipe is extra handy for anyone who is time-poor because the blueberries and spinach can be stored and used directly from frozen. This saves time and money because frozen produce is often cheaper without compromising on the nutritional profile.

BLUEBERRY THICKIE

Katie says: *"This is a favourite recommendation of mine to busy clients who need to fuel up for the day ahead without compromising on their nutrition. The recipe is flexible and forgiving so even the most kitchen-shy clients have had success with it! The smoothie is antioxidant-rich due to the blueberries and spinach, and the nut/seed butter provides essential fats. Oats also provide long-lasting energy and are a good source of fibre."*

METHOD

1. Place all the ingredients in a high-powered blender.
2. Blitz on high for about 30-45 seconds until smooth.
3. Pour into a glass to serve.

SERVES	TIME	PLANTS
1	3-4 mins	6

INGREDIENTS

- 2 handfuls (or 4 heaped tbsp) blueberries (fresh or frozen)
- Handful of baby spinach leaves (fresh or frozen)
- 20g porridge oats
- 1 tbsp smooth almond butter
- 1 tbsp chia seeds
- ¼ tsp vanilla extract
- 250ml milk (any plant or dairy milk)
- 1 tsp ground cinnamon
- Scoop of vanilla protein powder (optional, whey or plant protein)

 SWAPS

Vegan and dairy-free: use plant milk and plant protein
Nut-free: use tahini or sunflower seed butter instead of almond butter
Gluten-free: use gluten-free oats

RECIPE BY KATIE SHORE

Katie is a registered nutritional therapist specialising in fertility, pregnancy and postnatal health. She supports women to be as healthy as possible so that they can have a baby, enjoy their pregnancy or recover from birth. She lives in Bedfordshire with her husband and son.

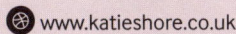 www.katieshore.co.uk 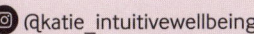 @katie_intuitivewellbeing

SERVES	TIME	PLANTS
3-4	50 mins	3

INGREDIENTS

- 1 large sweet potato, unpeeled but scrubbed clean, grated
- 1 tsp pink Himalayan salt or sea salt
- 4½ tbsp coconut or olive oil
- 1 large red or white onion, finely sliced or grated
- Handful of spinach leaves or ball of defrosted frozen spinach (or any green leaf you have to hand), roughly chopped
- 40g brown rice flour/gluten-free flour/plain flour

SWEET POTATO AND CARAMELISED ONION HASH

Catherine says: *"These are delicious as they are but can also be served with toppings such as: slices of dressed avocado (pinch of salt, drizzle of lemon juice and olive oil); a poached or fried egg; fresh herbs; baked beans; a drizzle of tahini; salad leaves; or chilli slices."*

METHOD

1. Preheat the oven to 200°C/180°C fan/gas mark 6.
2. In a bowl, mix the grated sweet potato with a pinch of salt, then set aside.
3. Gently warm 1 tbsp of oil in a shallow saucepan, turn up the heat and add the onion and a pinch of salt. Keep them on the move to coat nicely in the oil, turn the heat down and put a lid on to steam cook.
4. Once the onions have released their juices and are beginning to collapse, remove the lid. On a medium heat allow to caramelise, stirring occasionally so they don't burn. When jammy and sweet, transfer to a bowl to cool.
5. Remove any excess liquid from the sweet potato by squeezing it in handfuls between your fingers, then place it in the bowl with the caramelised onions.
6. Wilt the spinach in a hot pan with another ½ tbsp of coconut oil or olive oil and then add to the bowl with the onions. (If using defrosted frozen spinach, you don't need to wilt it, but will need to squeeze out the excess water.)
7. Add the remaining salt to the flour and mix well. Add this to the bowl with the onions, sweet potato and spinach and mix well.
8. Divide the mixture into 6-8 portions, depending on the size you want them. Squeeze each portion together so the mixture forms a ball and keep pressing until it begins to hold its shape.
9. Meanwhile, preheat the remaining oil in a baking tray. When at temperature, carefully roll each hash portion in the hot oil and spread them evenly on a baking sheet, leaving a gap around each hash. Press each one down slightly with the back of a flat spatula or a fork. Bake for 10 minutes. Then carefully turn each hash over, flattening down again, and bake for a further 10-15 minutes or until beginning to turn golden brown — you want both sides to be slightly caramelised. (Note: smaller hash may need less cooking time.)
10. Transfer to a piece of kitchen paper and pat off any excess oil.

RECIPE BY CATHERINE SHARMAN

Catherine, the visionary founder of Après Food, is a passionate and well-respected chef and a trained functional nutritionist. A graduate of the Institute for Optimum Nutrition (ION), she believes in the transformative power of good nutritionally-considered food and enjoying the foods you love. With her extensive expertise, Catherine crafts restaurant-quality, certified organic, home-cooked, frozen meals that are nutritionally functional and deeply satisfying for your body and mind.

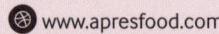 www.apresfood.com 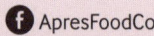 ApresFoodCo 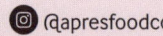 @apresfoodco

"Your gut microbiome is the sum of all your gut microbes and their DNA in your digestive tract. For the beneficial microbes to thrive, they need to be fed a variety of colourful polyphenols (compounds found in plant foods) such as veg, fruit, herbs and spices."

RAINBOW EGG MUFFINS

Jane says: *"My clients love these for an easy breakfast you can prepare in advance. They are a savoury breakfast, rich in protein that helps stabilise blood sugar through the day. The rainbow element of coloured veg helps to nourish your gut microbiome and pack in five different varieties of vegetables, herbs and spices in each muffin.*

"I find the temperature needed varies with individual ovens and the water content of your vegetables so adjust accordingly."

SERVES	TIME	PLANTS
12	30 mins	5+

METHOD

1. Preheat the oven to 190°C/170°C fan/gas mark 5. Either grease a muffin tin or use silicon muffin moulds.
2. Put the diced vegetables into a large bowl with the salt, pepper, herbs and spices.
3. Beat the eggs, add to the vegetables and mix well.
4. Divide the mixture between the muffin moulds and bake for 20 minutes.
5. Check the egg is cooked using a knife or toothpick.
6. Eat warm or leave to cool on a wire rack and then refrigerate.

INGREDIENTS

- 6 small handfuls (or 3 cups) vegetables (choose 3 types of seasonal veg from carrot, tomato, red/spring onion, bell pepper, asparagus, broccoli, spinach/kale, olives), diced
- ½ tsp each pink Himalayan salt or rock salt and freshly ground black pepper
- 1 tbsp fresh herbs (coriander, parsley or chives) or 1 tsp dried herbs (oregano or mixed herbs)
- 1 tsp dried spices (choose from paprika, turmeric, cumin)
- 6 eggs

⇆ SWAPS

Money-saving: use frozen veg
More protein: add small cubes of leftover/cooked meat or flaked salmon

RECIPE BY JANE BARRETT

Jane helps adults and children with digestive issues take control of their health through nutrition. Giving practical, realistic and inspiring advice, she loves to help her clients get confident in their food choices to keep their gut nurtured and calm.

 www.nurturingnutrition.co.uk NurturingNutritionLtd

SHAKSHUKA

SERVES	TIME	PLANTS
4	50 mins	7+

INGREDIENTS

- 2 tbsp coconut oil or olive oil
- 2 large onions, thinly sliced
- 2 red peppers, cut into long slices
- 2 yellow peppers, cut into long slices
- 2 garlic cloves, finely chopped
- ½ tsp cumin seeds
- ½ tsp smoked paprika
- 1 tbsp tomato or red pepper purée
- 1 x 690g jar tomato passata
- Salt and pepper to taste
- 4 free-range eggs
- Handful of fresh coriander, chopped (optional)
- Handful of fresh parsley, chopped (optional)
- 100g feta, crumbled (optional)

Nicki says: *"I love this shakshuka recipe, it's a quick and nutritious breakfast or lunch option, it tastes so good and it's very low carb. That means it's great for blood sugar balance, which supports energy, mood and weight management."*

METHOD

1. Heat the oil in a large pan, until melted (if using coconut oil) or hot (if using olive oil). Then add the onions and peppers and cook until soft — about 15 minutes.
2. Add the garlic, cumin and smoked paprika, and stir for a couple of minutes.
3. Add the tomato or red pepper purée, passata and seasoning, and simmer for at least 10 minutes.
4. Make 4 wells in the sauce. Add an egg to each well and cook on a medium-high heat until the whites are firm, but the yolks are still soft — about 10 minutes.
5. Sprinkle over herbs and feta if using and serve.

 SWAPS

Dairy-free: omit the feta or use a dairy-free alternative

RECIPE BY NICKI WILLIAMS

Nicki is an award-winning nutritionist, author and speaker, and a leading expert in women's health and hormones. She is the founder of Happy Hormones for Life, helping women of all ages to rebalance their hormones, reclaim their health and feel better than ever.

 www.happyhormonesforlife.com 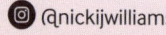 @nickijwilliams

> Coconut yoghurt is a great alternative to dairy yoghurt if you're sensitive to dairy or just fancy a change. It is lactose- and casein-free and naturally sweet and creamy. Coconut yoghurt is a probiotic-rich food packed with beneficial bacteria that can support digestion. Use it in recipes as you would Greek or natural yoghurt.

SPICY BURRITO BREAKFAST BOWL

SERVES	TIME	PLANTS
2	25 mins	15

Charlotte says: *"This savoury breakfast bowl is one of my favourites. It's packed with veggies and lean protein, and has a spicy kick. I encourage you to try this recipe if you would like to move away from traditional breakfast fare and challenge your ideas of what breakfast should look like."*

METHOD

1. Preheat the oven to 200°C/180°C fan/gas mark 6. Line a baking tray with parchment paper and place the fish on the tray.
2. Place the olive oil, cayenne pepper, cumin, coriander, salt and black pepper in a small jug and whisk to combine. Drizzle over the fish and cook for 12-15 minutes, or until cooked through.
3. Meanwhile, add the salsa ingredients to a small bowl and toss to combine.
4. Divide the cabbage, radishes, rice and salsa between serving bowls and top with the cooked fish. Add a dollop of coconut yoghurt and sprinkle with seeds to serve.

INGREDIENTS

- 2 x 150g skinless boneless cod fillets
- 1 tbsp extra virgin olive oil
- ¼ tsp cayenne pepper
- ½ tsp ground cumin
- ¼ tsp ground coriander
- Sea salt and cracked black pepper

For the salsa

- 1 ripe avocado, diced
- ½ small red onion, finely chopped
- ¼ fresh mango, diced
- ½ small cucumber, diced
- 2 tbsp chopped fresh coriander
- Juice of 1 lime
- ¼ tsp sea salt

For the salad

- ¼ each of red and white cabbage, shredded
- 4 radishes, finely sliced
- 250g cooked brown basmati rice
- 2 tbsp coconut yoghurt, to serve
- 2 tbsp pumpkin and sunflower seeds, to serve

RECIPE BY CHARLOTTE GRAND

Charlotte is a registered nutritional therapist, author of *The Fertility Kitchen* cookbook and creator of the popular Instagram channels @thefertilitykitchen and @themenopausekitchen where she shares her wholesome balanced approach alongside deliciously simple everyday recipes. Charlotte is passionate about helping women transform their health in preparation for conception, pregnancy, through perimenopause and beyond.

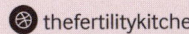 thefertilitykitchen.com   menopausekitchen.com   @thefertilitykitchen   @themenopausekitchen

Soups

SERVES | **TIME** | **PLANTS**
4 | 1 hr 10 mins | 10

INGREDIENTS

- 5 red peppers
- 2 tbsp olive oil
- 1 onion, finely diced
- 2 garlic cloves, crushed
- 1 tsp cumin seeds, ground
- 2 tsp smoked Spanish paprika, plus more to taste
- 200g dried red lentils, rinsed
- 1 x 400g tin chopped tomatoes
- 1.2 litres gluten-free vegetable stock
- 1 tsp fresh thyme leaves
- 2 tbsp fresh parsley, finely chopped
- Sea salt and black pepper to taste
- Juice of 1-2 lemons
- Swirl of extra virgin olive oil (optional, to serve)

ROASTED RED PEPPER SOUP

Alli says: *"I love to make this soup as it is both delicious and nutritious. It makes a perfect lunch and can be frozen in portions.*

"The red peppers, parsley and lemon juice make this recipe a great source of vitamin C; we need plenty of this antioxidant nutrient to support immunity. Vitamin C is also crucial for the production of collagen and is therefore important for our bone, cartilage and skin health."

METHOD

1. Preheat the oven to 180°C/160°C fan/gas mark 4.
2. In a baking tray lined with baking paper/parchment, roast the red peppers in the oven for 35-40 minutes.
3. Once out of the oven, put the peppers in a large bowl and cover with foil so they steam.
4. Allow to cool for 5 minutes, then remove skins and core/seeds and slice thinly.
5. Heat the olive oil in a pan and sauté the onion until soft. Add the garlic, cumin and paprika and briefly sauté before adding the lentils, tomatoes and stock. Simmer.
6. Add the peppers to the soup along with their juices from roasting; add the thyme leaves and continue to cook until the lentils start to break down. Cook for 20 minutes.
7. Optionally, blend the soup until smooth with a stick blender once cooked (or leave chunky if you prefer).
8. Stir in the parsley and season with salt, pepper and lemon juice. You can add some extra paprika if desired and a swirl of extra virgin olive oil as you serve.

⇄ **SWAPS**

Timesaving: use a jar of roasted red peppers instead of cooking them yourself, to save 45 minutes

---

RECIPE BY ALLI GODBOLD

Alli qualified from the Institute for Optimum Nutrition (ION) back in 1996, and for over 25 years has practised as a nutritional therapist in West London and more recently in Wiltshire and Somerset. Alli specialises in weight loss and fatigue as well as digestive and hormonal health. Her most recent book, *Feed Your Health 2*, can be purchased from Amazon and her website.

 www.feedyourhealth.co.uk 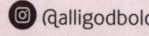 @alligodbold

ROASTED TOMATO AND BASIL SOUP

Janie says: *"This is one of my favourites because it's so easy to make but also really delicious. Tomatoes contain a powerful antioxidant called lycopene which helps the body mop up harmful free radicals — and it happens to be more potent when cooked. So, the soup is also super nutritious!"*

SERVES	TIME	PLANTS
4	40-50 mins	5

METHOD

1. Preheat the oven to 200°C/180°C fan/gas mark 6.
2. Spread the tomatoes, onions and garlic over one or two roasting trays. Add the basil, leaving a few pieces aside for garnish. Drizzle over the olive oil.
3. Cover the bottom of the tray with vegetable stock (at least 2.5cm deep).
4. Cook in the oven for approximately 30 minutes, until the tomatoes are soft and have released their juices. Check halfway through and give the contents of the tray a good stir to avoid burning.
5. Remove the vegetables from the oven and allow to cool. Squeeze the flesh out of the garlic cloves and discard the skins.
6. Put the roasted vegetables into a food processor and blitz everything together (or tip into a pan and blitz with a hand blender).
7. Add the remaining stock until the soup reaches a desired consistency.
8. If needed, return the soup to a pan to warm.
9. Season with salt and pepper. Serve with a swirl of crème fraîche or a non-dairy alternative, a few extra torn basil leaves, and 1-2 tbsp pumpkin seeds.

INGREDIENTS

- 2kg ripe tomatoes, halved or quartered (beef, plum, cherry or a mixture)
- 3 onions, cut into wedges
- 4 garlic cloves, unpeeled
- 1 bunch of basil leaves, torn
- 100ml olive oil
- 500ml gluten-free vegetable stock
- Sea salt and black pepper
- Crème fraîche or a non-dairy alternative, to serve
- Pumpkin seeds, to serve

⇄ SWAPS

Vegan and dairy-free: replace the crème fraîche with a non-dairy alternative such as unsweetened soya yoghurt or coconut yoghurt

RECIPE BY JANIE PERRY

Janie is a registered nutritional therapy practitioner specialising in weight management and sports nutrition. She is also a registered homeopath. Janie is passionate about helping others eat better to feel better and perform better with simple and easy to follow advice.

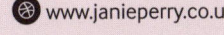 www.janieperry.co.uk   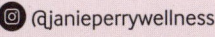 @janieperrywellness

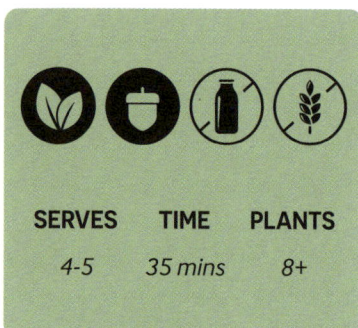

SERVES 4-5

TIME 35 mins

PLANTS 8+

CREAMY CHESTNUT SOUP

Karine says: *"Enrich your dinner with this creamy and diverse vegetable and chestnut soup. The harmonious blend of curry powder, ginger and garlic, combined with the nutty sweetness of chestnuts, creates a range of flavours in every spoonful. To top it off, the smooth, protein-rich silken tofu provides a luxurious creaminess that unites these ingredients in perfect balance. This comforting dish is not only ideal for chilly days or cozy nights, but also serves as a wholesome and flavourful option to nourish your body and soul."*

INGREDIENTS

- 1 litre gluten-free vegetable broth
- 2 onions, chopped
- 2 garlic cloves, minced
- 1 tbsp curry powder, mild or medium
- 2 tsp fresh ginger, grated
- 2 medium leeks, chopped
- 2 medium potatoes, chopped
- 180g vacuum-packed chestnuts (e.g. Merchant Gourmet)
- 300g silken tofu
- Salt and pepper, to season (optional)
- Handful of chestnuts, chopped (optional, to serve)
- Handful of chopped fresh herbs, such as parsley or coriander (optional, to serve)

METHOD

1. Heat 250ml of the vegetable broth in a large pan.
2. Add the onions and cook for 5 minutes.
3. Stir in the garlic, curry powder and ginger, and cook for 2 minutes.
4. Add the remaining broth, leeks, potatoes and chestnuts and bring to a boil.
5. Cover and simmer for 20 minutes.
6. Blend the soup, then add the silken tofu and blend again until smooth and creamy. Optionally, season with salt and pepper to taste.
7. Garnish the soup with chestnuts and herbs (if using) before serving.

⇆ **SWAPS**

Soy intolerance/allergy: replace silken tofu with double cream, thickened with cornflour

RECIPE BY KARINE STEPHAN

Karine is a registered nutritional therapy practitioner specialising in women's health, with a particular interest in hormone health, as well as ADHD. Her passion is to support women to make positive, sustainable changes through diet and lifestyle. Karine loves experimenting with food and helped her husband start Palace Culture, an award-winning plant-based cheese alternative company.

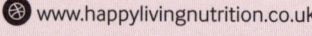 www.happylivingnutrition.co.uk 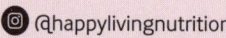 @happylivingnutrition

> Tofu and miso are a good source of protein, and are fermented foods used by many cultures around the world for their health promoting qualities. Research suggests that these foods may have a beneficial impact on gut health.

TOFU AND VEGETABLE MISO SOUP

Safia says: *"This is my own go-to comfort food. It's warming and I know it contains an abundance of nutrients. I do recommend it to clients and at workshops because you don't need a huge amount of time and there are no chef skills required – equipment is one knife, one pan and two bowls for a meal that satisfies. I particularly recommend this to new vegans or vegetarians as I find the protein element of a meal is often forgotten and other options may sometimes be a bit carbohydrate heavy."*

SERVES	TIME	PLANTS
2-4	30 mins	10+

METHOD

1. In a medium-sized saucepan, heat the olive oil and gently fry the spring onions, garlic and ginger. Add the turmeric and chilli (if using) and continue to fry for a couple of minutes.
2. Stir in the celery and tofu and gently fry for another 2 minutes. Add a small amount of the stock if needed.
3. Stir in the mushrooms, courgette, broccoli and kale.
4. Add the stock, bring to the boil, then simmer for 10-15 minutes.
5. Remove from the heat and stir in miso paste, until dissolved.

INGREDIENTS

- 1 tbsp olive oil
- 2 spring onions, sliced
- 1 large garlic clove, finely chopped
- 2.5cm piece fresh ginger, finely chopped
- ½ tsp ground turmeric
- Pinch of chilli powder (optional)
- 1 stick celery, sliced
- Half a packet of firm tofu, diced
- 2 large mushrooms, chopped into bitesize pieces
- 1 medium courgette, chopped into bitesize pieces
- 4 broccoli florets, sliced into smaller pieces
- 1 large curly kale leaf, torn into bitesize pieces
- 600ml gluten-free vegetable stock
- 1-2 tbsp gluten-free miso paste

⇄ SWAPS

Soya allergy: replace tofu with chicken, turkey, beans or lentils, and swap miso for chickpea miso or fish sauce
Celery allergy: replace with a vegetable of your choice
Higher carb: add noodles (rice noodles if gluten-free)
Flavour change: Replace the spices with herbs like parsley. The recipe was designed to use miso, ginger and turmeric as the base for the flavouring, but it can easily be adapted for a simpler vegetable soup

RECIPE BY SAFIA SAWAL

Safia graduated from the Institute for Optimum Nutrition (ION) in 2005 and has worked as a nutritional therapist ever since. As well as private practice, she has enjoyed bringing optimum nutrition to a wider audience through corporate work, workshops for charities and community groups, and as a clinic assessor for the University of Worcester's MSc Nutritional Therapy.

SERVES **TIME** **PLANTS**

3-4 45 mins 13+

INGREDIENTS

- 1 red chilli
- 1 tbsp olive oil
- 1 red onion, finely chopped
- 1 red pepper, cubed
- 150g cherry tomatoes, halved
- 2 garlic cloves, minced
- 1 bay leaf
- 2 sprigs of thyme, left whole
- 2 tsp gluten-free Mexican spice mix or DIY spice mix (plus extra for seasoning)
- ½ tsp cinnamon
- 3 sprigs of coriander
- 2 fresh unwaxed limes: zest of one, juice of two
- 2 x 400g tins black beans, drained
- 400ml gluten-free vegetable stock
- Freshly ground black pepper and sea salt to taste
- 2-3 tbsp natural yoghurt, to serve
- 1 ripe avocado, sliced, to serve

MEXICAN BLACK BEAN SOUP

Diana says: *"Mexican black bean soup is one of my favourite dishes. I regularly recommend it to my clients. It is nutritious and delicious without breaking the bank, and perfect for batch cooking. Black beans are packed with gut-health-promoting fibre, minerals, polyphenols and plant protein. Along with all the other diverse and colourful ingredients, this dish is a true feast for your microbes."*

METHOD

1. Deseed and finely slice half the chilli for the salsa; the other half is for the soup – keep it intact if you're going to remove it later.
2. Heat the olive oil over a medium heat in a medium-sized pot. Keep ½ tbsp of the onions for the salsa and fry the rest with the red pepper for 4-5 minutes.
3. Add the tomatoes, garlic, bay leaf, thyme sprigs, spice mix, cinnamon and chilli and simmer covered at low heat for 10 minutes.
4. In the meantime, set aside a few coriander leaves for garnish, and finely chop the rest including the stems. To make the salsa, mix the lime juice, lime zest, chopped coriander, leftover red onion, sliced chilli and a pinch of salt.
5. Add the beans and vegetable stock to the soup pot and simmer at medium heat for 15-20 minutes. Season to taste with 1-2 tsp of lime salsa, spice mix, salt and pepper.
6. Remove the thyme sprigs from the pot and, optionally, remove the chilli if you prefer it less spicy. Then blend the soup with a hand blender, so that it is creamy but still chunky.
7. Serve the soup topped with yoghurt, avocado slices, lime salsa and fresh coriander leaves.

⇆ **SWAPS**

Vegan and dairy-free: omit yoghurt or use vegan yoghurt
Probiotic: replace yoghurt with kefir

DIY SPICE MIX

- ½ tsp cumin • ½ tsp sweet paprika
- ¼ tsp dried oregano • ¼ tsp chilli powder (or more to taste) • ¼ tsp smoked paprika
- ¼ tsp onion and garlic powder (optional)
- pinch of cayenne (optional)

RECIPE BY DIANA WARRINGS

After graduating from the Institute for Optimum Nutrition (ION) in 2016, Diana went down the culinary nutrition route. She took further training at Leiths School of Food and Wine, and Hofmann Culinary School in Barcelona, and has been working as a holistic chef, recipe developer and content producer ever since. Diana runs a clinic in Berlin and leads cooking workshops.

 www.dianawarrings.com   @dianawarrings_nutrition

> Dietary fibre is a major food source for our gut microbes. They ferment the fibre and produce short-chain fatty acids, which act as a main source of energy for the cells in the gut lining and hence promote gut health. Too much fibre may cause bloating, excess gas or constipation, especially if you are not used to eating fibre, in which case it is better to start with smaller amounts.

BUTTERNUT SQUASH SOUP

Petronella says: *"This recipe feels like comfort food. The soup can be enjoyed hot, or cooked and cooled in the summer. Cooking renders vegetables more digestible than a smoothie, and almost any vegetables can be substituted for the ones in the recipe – and you can experiment with different herbs. The soup is suitable for anyone wanting to do a vegetable cleanse, or can be enjoyed as a meal with a protein accompaniment (chicken, pulses or tofu work well)."*

SERVES	TIME	PLANTS
6	25 mins	7

METHOD

1. Add the butternut squash, courgette, onion, garlic, rosemary and stock to a large pan.
2. Season well with salt and pepper and bring to the boil. Then simmer until the squash is tender – about 15 minutes.
3. Stir in the spinach until it wilts.
4. Optionally, blend for a smooth soup.
5. Divide into six portions and sprinkle with fresh herbs of your choice.

INGREDIENTS

- 400g butternut squash, peeled and diced
- 300g courgette, roughly chopped
- 1 onion, roughly chopped
- 2 garlic cloves, crushed (smoked garlic is great if you can find it)
- 1 tsp dried rosemary
- 800ml gluten-free vegetable or chicken stock/broth
- Salt and freshly ground black pepper
- 100g spinach leaves
- Handful of chopped fresh herbs, such as parsley or rosemary, to serve

⇄ SWAPS

Vegan: use vegetable stock/broth
Higher protein: add a tin or packet of cooked lentils or some chopped, cooked meat or tofu

RECIPE BY PETRONELLA RAVENSHEAR

After many years in clinical practice, Petronella created The Human Being Diet (HBD) as a healthy, easy to follow and anti-inflammatory eating programme for everyone who cares about their current and future health. Her books enable people to learn how to tune in and listen to the language of their body, whether they want to lose weight or not. Both of Petronella's books, *The Human Being Diet* (second edition) and *The HBD Cookbook*, can be found on Amazon.

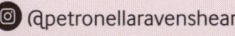 thehumanbeingdiet.com @petronellaravenshear

SERVES   **TIME**   **PLANTS**

1   5-20 mins   0-5

INGREDIENTS

- 350-400ml chicken, beef or vegetable stock
- 1 crushed garlic clove (optional)
- Pinch of chilli flakes (optional)
- 2.5cm piece fresh ginger, grated or sliced (optional)
- Handful of mushrooms, fresh or from frozen, thinly sliced (optional)
- 3-4 eggs (3 if using chicken or beef stock, 4 for veggie option)
- Approx. 1 tbsp soy sauce or tamari (optional, to season)
- 1 tsp miso paste (optional)
- Salt or liquid aminos to taste (optional, to season)
- Black or white pepper to taste (optional, to season)
- 1 chilli, sliced (optional, to garnish)
- 1 spring onion, finely sliced (optional, to garnish)

EGG DROP SOUP

Heather says: *"This soup is nutrient dense, high in protein, quick, easy and accessible with the possibility for infinite tweaks. It can be eaten any time of day and it's useful for those who are trying to optimise their protein intake but don't feel like eating very much, or as a post-workout meal. You can freeze leftover stock in soup-size portions or in large ice cube trays; stock can be cooked from frozen. Add leftover meat and veggies before adding the eggs for a more substantial soup."*

METHOD

1. In a small saucepan, combine the stock with your choice of seasonings (garlic, chilli flakes, ginger) and mushrooms, if using.
2. Bring to a boil and simmer for 3 minutes to infuse the flavours, or 8-10 minutes if using mushrooms.
3. Beat the eggs well in a bowl. Bring the broth back to a boil, and slowly pour in the beaten eggs, stirring to encourage a ribbon texture. The egg will cook almost instantly.
4. Season to taste with your choice of soy sauce, tamari, miso, salt, liquid aminos and black or white pepper. Optionally garnish with sliced chilli and spring onion. Eat while hot.

 SWAPS

Vegetarian: use vegetable stock
Gluten-free: Ensure the stock is gluten-free. If using, use tamari instead of soy sauce and gluten-free miso

RECIPE BY HEATHER ROSA

Heather is the Dean of the Institute for Optimum Nutrition (ION). Her mantra is "nutrient-dense, natural food is medicine for mind, body and spirit". Interested in ancestral and traditional diets, Heather is a nose-to-tail eating enthusiast who prioritises fat and protein in her diet for optimal post-menopausal brain and musculoskeletal health.

 www.linkedin.com/in/heather-rosa-3a84871b

Bone broth

Egg drop soup

SERVES | **TIME** | **PLANTS**
8 | 2 hr 10 mins + | 3

BONE BROTH

Jenny says: *"Lots of us benefit from consuming bone broth, especially when we are looking for benefits to gut health and skin/bone health, but for some it creates a problem with histamine. This pressure-cooked method makes a lower histamine version."*

INGREDIENTS

- 500g organic/grass-fed bones
- 3 carrots, unpeeled
- 3 celery sticks
- 1 onion, peeled and halved
- 1 tbsp apple cider vinegar
- 2 tsp salt
- 3 litres water (or to the fill line in your pot)

METHOD

1. Place all ingredients into a multicooker such as Instant Pot or Ninja Foodi and cook on high pressure for 2 hours. Leave to release pressure naturally at the end of cooking.
2. Strain off the broth from the cooked veggies and discard the veggies.
3. Leave the broth to cool in the pot and keep in the fridge overnight.
4. Skim off the hardened fat on the surface to reveal the gelatinous broth below.
5. Use the broth in soups, stews and risottos.

ON THE HOB

You can make a higher histamine version of this recipe on the hob if you don't own a multicooker. Fill the pot to cover the bones (because you need more water when cooking this on the hob due to evaporation) and cook for 12 hours on the smallest hob ring on the lowest setting. Then follow instructions 2-5 above. (You may need to add a little extra water during cooking so keep checking the pot to ensure it is not drying out.)

RECIPE BY JENNY TSCHIESCHE

Jenny is a *Sunday Times* No.1 bestselling author and has written several cookbooks. Besides her books, Jenny also sees clients, delivers workshops, works with schools and athletes, and partners with companies such as supermarkets, all in her capacity as a nutritional therapist.

 www.jennytschiesche.com 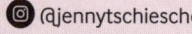 @jennytschiesche

HOW TO MAKE DELICIOUS SOUP FROM LEFTOVERS IN YOUR KITCHEN

CHOOSE YOUR BASE
(up to 3)

- Onion, finely chopped
- Celery, finely chopped
- Carrots, diced
- Leeks, thinly sliced

AROMATICS
(as many as you like)

- Garlic cloves, crushed or minced
- Fresh ginger, minced
- Seeds, e.g. cumin, mustard, coriander

CHOOSE YOUR VEGETABLES
(1-3)

- Root vegetables, peeled and cubed, e.g. carrot, sweet potato, celeriac, butternut squash, parsnip
- Nightshades, chopped, e.g. tomato, aubergine, bell pepper
- Brassicas, chopped, e.g. broccoli, cauliflower, cabbage, kale
- Bulb vegetables, chopped, e.g. kohlrabi, fennel, leek
- Legumes, from tins or frozen, e.g. peas, sweetcorn
- Any other vegetable in your kitchen

BULK IT UP WITH SOME PROTEIN
(choose 1)

- Leftover cooked chicken, ripped
- Leftover cooked ham, cut into small cubes
- Beans or chickpeas, tinned
- Lentils, of any variety, tinned or dried (add extra water)
- Extra-firm tofu, cubed

CHOOSE YOUR LIQUIDS
(1 or 2)

- Stock or broth
- Tomato (purée, passata or tinned)
- Double cream
- Silken tofu, blended until creamy
- Coconut milk or cream

ADD SOME FLAVOUR
(as many as you like)

- Salt and pepper
- Fresh herbs, roughly chopped, e.g. mint, dill, chives, parsley, coriander
- Ground spices, e.g. cumin, smoked paprika, coriander, turmeric
- Dried herbs, e.g. sage, oregano, rosemary, thyme, bay leaf
- Jars or bottles, e.g. miso, soy sauce, vinegar
- Chilli (any)

METHOD

1. Put your preferred oil in a large pot on the hob and heat for a couple of minutes.
2. Add your base ingredients, e.g. onion and celery, and cook for a couple of minutes, stirring continuously. Then add your aromatics, e.g. garlic, and cook until everything has softened, stirring continuously.
3. Add your vegetables and cook for 5 minutes, while stirring, until slightly softened. Alternatively, speed up this process by using leftover cooked vegetables.
4. Add your protein ingredients and give everything a stir for a couple of minutes.
5. Add your stock or broth, if using – a generous splash of boiling water if not – and turn up the heat until the liquid boils. Turn the heat back down to low and simmer with the lid on for 15 minutes, or until your ingredients are cooked.
6. Then, thicken your soup with another liquid, e.g. cream, tomato or silken tofu. At this point, you may wish to blend your soup, if that's your preferred texture.
7. Taste your soup. Add flavourings, tasting as you go, until you like it – then step away! If you're not sure what will taste nice, decant a little of your soup into a small bowl and experiment on a miniature scale before adding anything to your big pot.
8. Are you happy with the texture of your soup? If it's too thick, add water. If it's too runny, decant a little into a bowl, add a little cornflour, and whisk until smooth to make a paste; add this back to your soup to thicken it up.
9. When you're happy with your soup, give everything a final stir and bring up the heat until it bubbles. Serve with crusty bread, buttered toast, croutons or anything else you like, and garnish as desired, e.g. with a drizzle of cream or olive oil, a sprig of fresh herbs, or a sprinkle of seeds.

Salads

MANGO, HALLOUMI AND SPINACH SALAD

Sue says: *"I love this recipe for summer lunches. It is quick and easy to make, colourful, uplifting and packed with nutrients. As well as adding flavour, the lemon and apple cider vinegar may also help support digestion. The recipe is really flexible too, and I sometimes like to be extra generous with the ingredients so I have enough for the next day!"*

SERVES	TIME	PLANTS
4	20 mins	10

METHOD

1. Arrange the spinach and watercress on a large plate/dish.
2. Scatter over the tomatoes, avocado, onion and mango.
3. Place a frying pan over a medium heat and dry-fry the pine nuts for 3-5 minutes until golden, stirring occasionally. Set aside.
4. In a bowl, mix the cubed halloumi with half the olive oil and the chilli flakes, ensuring the halloumi is evenly coated.
5. Heat the remaining oil in a frying pan over a medium heat. When hot, add the halloumi and cook for approximately 4 minutes, turning half way, until golden.
6. Meanwhile, prepare the dressing by mixing all the ingredients together in a bowl.
7. Add the warm halloumi and pine nuts to the salad and pour over the dressing.
8. Sprinkle over the pomegranate seeds.

INGREDIENTS

- 3 large handfuls spinach
- 2 handfuls watercress
- Punnet of cherry tomatoes, halved
- 2 avocados, scooped out and sliced
- 1 red onion, sliced
- 1 mango, peeled and cubed
- Handful of pine nuts
- 1 pack halloumi, cubed
- 1 tbsp olive oil or avocado oil
- 2 tsp chilli flakes
- 2 tbsp pomegranate seeds

For the salad dressing

- 3 tbsp virgin olive oil
- 1 tbsp apple cider vinegar
- Squeeze of raw honey
- Squeeze of lemon

⇆ SWAPS

Vegan: swap halloumi for vegan cheese or tofu, and honey for maple syrup (about ½ tsp)
Dairy-free: swap halloumi for non-dairy cheese, cooked meat, fish or tofu
Nut-free: omit the pine nuts or swap for pumpkin seeds

RECIPE BY SUE EVANS

Sue is a registered nutritional therapy practitioner and head of the CPD department at the Institute for Optimum Nutrition (ION). In her private practice, Sue Evans Nutrition, Sue supports clients with a range of health concerns, including hormonal, digestive and stress-related issues. She also has a general interest in cancer, pyroluria and endometriosis. Sue is a member of The British Society of Integrative Oncology.

 www.sueevansnutrition.co.uk   @sueevansnutrition

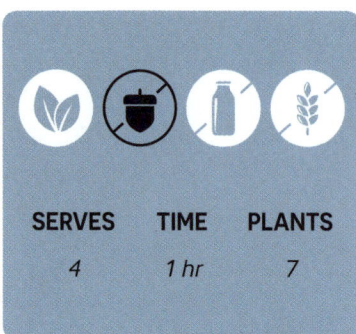

SERVES 4

TIME 1 hr

PLANTS 7

INGREDIENTS

- 1 vegetable stock cube
- 125ml boiling water
- 100g dry wholemeal couscous
- 1 tbsp honey
- 1 tbsp sriracha
- 1 tsp balsamic vinegar
- 200g halloumi, sliced
- 1 large cauliflower, chopped into small florets
- 1 x 400g tin chickpeas, drained and rinsed
- 1 tbsp paprika, sweet or smoked
- 1 tbsp harissa
- 1 tbsp olive oil
- 1 red onion, chopped
- Handful of rocket and/or spinach
- Handful of feta, crumbled

HONEY HALLOUMI AND CRISPY CHICKPEA SALAD

Rachel says: *"Preparation is key for busy clients looking to eat well whilst remaining energised throughout the day. I love this recipe because it's packed with blood sugar-balancing nutrients, it can be eaten hot or cold, and it's the perfect lunch, mid-afternoon snack or dinner during a busy working day."*

METHOD

1. Preheat the oven to 200°C/180°C fan/gas mark 6.
2. Add a stock cube to 125ml of boiling water in a bowl and stir. Add the couscous and cover. Set aside.
3. In a bowl, mix the honey, sriracha and balsamic vinegar. Add the sliced halloumi and mix well, ensuring the halloumi is well coated with the mixture. Set aside whilst preparing the remaining ingredients.
4. Put the cauliflower and chickpeas into a roasting tin. Add the paprika, harissa and olive oil and mix until evenly coated. Spread evenly onto the tray and roast for 30-45 minutes, checking them regularly as oven temperatures can vary. Turn halfway through cooking. Add the red onion to the roasting tin for the last 20 minutes.
5. Once the vegetables are almost ready, pan fry the marinated halloumi on a medium-high heat for a couple of minutes on each side, until golden, or air fry for 5 minutes at 160°C on each side.
6. Once everything is prepared, toss the couscous and then spoon onto a serving dish. Add the roasted cauliflower, chickpeas, red onion and rocket, and lay the halloumi on top. Crumble over the feta and then drizzle some honey, sriracha and balsamic over the dish.

 **SWAPS**

Vegan and dairy-free: swap the halloumi with tofu and omit the feta or use a vegan alternative. For vegan, replace the honey with agave
Gluten-free: use quinoa instead of couscous and ensure the stock cube is gluten-free

RECIPE BY RACHEL REES

Rachel is a registered nutritional therapist who is passionate about educating and empowering clients to achieve optimal health through the power of nutrition. She believes that exploring new recipes and experimenting with high quality ingredients is not only a rewarding process but allows us to appreciate the nutritional value of food.

 www.rachelreesnutrition.com 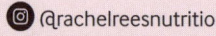 @rachelreesnutrition

"
Level up this recipe
by pairing it with an
additional source of
protein i.e. chicken, fish
or tofu, to supercharge
your satiety.
"

WARM LENTIL AND GOAT'S CHEESE SALAD

Lorna says: *"This is one of my favourite lentil dishes because puy lentils are quick to cook and do not need soaking. Lentils are rich in nutrients, high in fibre and an excellent low glycaemic index food. They can be eaten warm or cold as a salad, with a little dressing added and some mixed salad leaves."*

SERVES	TIME	PLANTS
2-4	35 mins	10

METHOD

1. Put the lentils, carrot, celery and herbs into a large saucepan and cover with cold water. Bring to the boil then cover the pan and simmer for about 15-20 minutes until the lentils are just tender.
2. Meanwhile, heat the olive oil in a medium non-stick frying pan, add the onion and cook for 2-3 minutes until they begin to soften; then add the sliced leeks and garlic and stir-fry for 5 minutes, until just tender.
3. Drain the lentils, discard the bay leaf and thyme sprigs (if using), and put into a bowl. Add the leeks, garlic, onion, tomatoes and parsley.
4. In a small bowl, whisk the extra virgin olive oil and vinegar together with a little salt and freshly ground black pepper. Pour this over the lentil salad and toss together.
5. Divide the salad between serving plates and top with the goat's cheese.

INGREDIENTS

- 250g puy lentils
- 1 large carrot, diced
- 1 large stalk celery, finely chopped
- 1 bay leaf
- 3 sprigs thyme or 1 tsp dried thyme
- 1 tbsp olive oil
- 1 small red onion, chopped
- 2 medium leeks (approx. 350g), sliced
- 1 large garlic clove, finely chopped
- 2 large vine tomatoes, chopped
- 3 tbsp fresh parsley, chopped
- 2 tbsp extra virgin olive oil
- 1 tbsp balsamic vinegar
- Salt and black pepper to taste
- 100g pack soft goat's cheese, roughly chopped

⇆ SWAPS

Vegan and dairy-free: replace the goat's cheese with tofu or a dairy-free cheese

RECIPE BY LORNA RHODES

Lorna trained as a home economist and worked as a cookery writer and food stylist for 40 years, creating recipes for books, food companies and PR campaigns. She always promoted healthy eating and then chose to study nutritional therapy. Lorna loves working with clients to improve their health with dietary changes.

 www.nutritiondynamics.co.uk 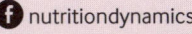 nutritiondynamics

SERVES | **TIME** | **PLANTS**
4-6 | 55 mins | 13

INGREDIENTS

- 200g butternut squash, cut into cubes
- 200g cauliflower, broken into small florets
- 2 tbsp olive oil
- 1 tbsp cumin seeds
- 2 tsp turmeric
- Salt and pepper to taste
- 100g brazil nuts
- 200g brown rice
- 1 garlic clove, crushed
- 100g green lentils, dried
- 1 large red onion, chopped
- 200g pomegranate seeds
- Handful of fresh dill, chopped
- 200g feta, crumbled

For the salad dressing

- Juice of 1 large orange
- 2 tbsp pomegranate molasses
- 3 tbsp date paste or 2 tsp honey, syrup or date molasses
- Salt to taste

MEDITERRANEAN RICE AND LENTIL BOWL

Belén says: *"This dish is great for those who tend to skip lunch during workdays due to time constraints. It can be made in large quantities and kept in the fridge for a few days. It is particularly rich in plant fibre, folate, B6 and antioxidants, all of which are hormone-balancing nutrients. Overall: nutritious, tasty, versatile and easy to make."*

METHOD

1. Heat the oven to 200°C/180°C fan/gas mark 6 and line a baking tray with baking parchment.
2. Place the butternut squash and cauliflower on the baking tray and drizzle with the olive oil. Scatter on the cumin seeds, dust with turmeric, and season generously with salt and pepper. Use your hands to ensure that every piece is coated. Roast for 30-35 minutes until both cauliflower and butternut squash are tender. After 20 minutes, add the brazil nuts to roast with them. After the full 30-35 minutes, remove from the oven and leave to cool down.
3. Once the vegetables are in the oven, brown the dry rice in a saucepan on the hob with the garlic in a little olive oil for 5 minutes. Cover with water, add salt, and leave to simmer. Then, in a separate pan with a lid, cover the lentils with water and bring to the boil. Leave both the rice and lentils to cook for 20-30 minutes until tender. When done, give them a quick rinse under cold water to bring them to room temperature and stop them from further cooking. This will allow them to stay tender but firm.
4. In a large bowl, toss the cooked rice and lentils; roasted cauliflower, butternut squash and brazil nuts; red onion, pomegranate and dill.
5. Combine the dressing ingredients in a bowl then pour over the tossed ingredients and mix well. Serve with the feta crumbled over the top.

 SWAPS

Vegan: swap feta for a vegan alternative; don't use honey in the dressing
Dairy-free: use a dairy-free alternative to feta
Nut-free: omit brazil nuts; optionally replace with 100g chickpeas

RECIPE BY BELÉN VÁZQUEZ

Belén helps parents build strong healthy foundations for their children. Her Gut Health programme provides natural solutions for gut, mood and behavioural issues. Belén graduated from the Institute for Optimum Nutrition (ION) and holds an MSc in Personalised Nutrition from CNELM. She loves creating tasty and nutritious recipes for the whole family.

 www.belenoptimumhealth.com belenoptimumhealth @belenoptimumhealth belenvazquez-optimumhealth

Try experimenting with different vegetables according to availability or season (e.g. beetroot, pumpkin, parsnip, courgette) and different wholegrains (e.g. quinoa, pearl barley, red rice)

"

From an environmental and nutritional standpoint, wild fish is the better choice for this salmon niçoise dish. Farmed salmon tends to be fed a processed fish feed, compared to the vertebrates that are consumed by wild fish. The result of this is that the omega-6 fat content in farmed fish is higher, while the calcium and iron content is lower. However, the bigger concern highlighted by environmentalists is the potential contaminants and antibiotics in farmed fish.

"

SALMON NIÇOISE

Kirstie says: *"This dish is so versatile. Much like a traditional nicoise, you can also add some boiled egg to this dish. I sometimes roast baby potatoes, rather than boil them. I also use whatever green vegetables I have in my fridge, focusing on what is in season.*

"I'm a pescatarian and I love a summer salad, so this dish ticks every box. It contains lots of delicious plants and is ideal for a summer evening."

SERVES	TIME	PLANTS
4	1 hr	8+

METHOD

1. Preheat the oven to 180°C/160°C fan/gas mark 4.
2. Place the salmon onto an oiled baking tray and cover with tinfoil. Bake for 20 minutes then set aside to cool.
3. Boil the new potatoes until cooked – about 15 minutes. Leave to cool.
4. Steam the green beans and asparagus until just cooked – about 3 minutes. Leave to cool.
5. In a large bowl, mix the salad leaves, sliced onion, sliced pepper and olives.
6. Heat the butter and oil in a large frying pan, and toss the new potatoes, asparagus and green beans until warmed through. Leave to cool for 2-3 minutes, then stir through the salad leaves.
7. In a small bowl, whisk the dressing ingredients together and pour over the salad. Toss gently.
8. To serve, place the salmon on top of the salad and sprinkle over the chives.

⇆ SWAPS

Dairy-free: *"Tossing the potatoes, asparagus and green beans in a little salted butter adds a layer of decadence, but this step could be avoided for those who want to keep the dish butter-free."*

People with IBS or IBD might want to lightly fry the onion before using
If you don't like salmon, use trout or fresh tuna instead
Swap the onion with spring onion if you prefer

INGREDIENTS

- 4 salmon fillets
- 200g new potatoes, washed
- 200g green beans, topped and tailed
- 200g asparagus
- Large bag of mixed salad leaves
- 1 onion, finely sliced
- 1 green pepper, finely sliced
- 100g niçoise olives (or other good quality black olives)
- 30g salted butter
- 10g olive oil
- 30g chives, freshly chopped

For the classic French dressing

- 100g olive oil
- 50g balsamic vinegar
- ½ tsp Dijon mustard
- ½ tsp sugar
- Salt and pepper to taste

RECIPE BY DR KIRSTIE LAWTON

Kirstie has been a paediatric nutritionist for 24 years and works predominantly with brain-related health conditions, as well as gut health and immune health-related concerns. She also has a special interest in adults with neurodegenerative conditions such as Parkinson's disease, Huntingdon's disease and motor neurone disease (MND).

 www.younutritionclinic.com www.nutritionandthebrain.com 📷 @drkirstielawton 📷 @nutritionandthebrain

ROAST CHICKEN RAINBOW SALAD WITH MAPLE AND TAHINI DRESSING

	SERVES	TIME	PLANTS
	4-6	2 hr	6-30

INGREDIENTS

For the chicken

- Whole chicken, or 4-6 chicken thighs/breasts
- Pink or sea salt and ground black pepper to taste
- 1 whole lemon
- Small handful of fresh thyme, leaves of approx. 3 sprigs removed and chopped; a couple more sprigs left whole
- Up to 1 tbsp extra virgin olive oil, for drizzling
- Approx. 100ml water

For the dressing

- 6 tbsp tahini
- 6 tbsp cold water (less if you would like a thicker sauce)
- 1 garlic clove (more if you would like it)
- Pinch of pink or sea salt
- 3 tsp olive oil
- 3 tsp coconut blossom or maple syrup

Chopped rainbow salad (all ingredients optional; choose as many as you wish, but include some salad leaves)

- Up to 100g rocket
- Up to 100g watercress
- 1 head chicory, thinly sliced
- 1 red bell pepper, finely sliced
- 150g cherry tomatoes, quartered
- ⅓ cucumber, sliced into thin batons
- 150g grated carrot (about 2 carrots)
- 1 avocado, sliced
- 20g salad cress
- 50g sweetcorn
- 50g mange tout, raw
- 50g red and white cabbage, raw and finely sliced

METHOD

1. Preheat the oven to 180°C/160°C fan/gas mark 4.
2. Put the chicken into a baking dish – big enough to fit, but not too big. Sprinkle with salt and pepper to taste.
3. Cut the lemon in half and squeeze the juice over the chicken, then sprinkle over some thyme leaves. Add the lemon halves and thyme sprigs to the dish, in the cavity if using a whole chicken.
4. Drizzle a little olive oil over the chicken.
5. Pour a glug of water into the baking dish. This helps keep the chicken moist and gives some lovely juices to add to gravy for another dish.
6. Cook your chicken according to packet instructions. Use a temperature probe to check the thickest part of the chicken breast and legs, so you are confident it is cooked. Then allow to cool.
7. Meanwhile, blend the dressing ingredients and adjust to taste. It will eventually go white and very smooth.
8. Once the chicken has cooled, 'rip' the chicken meat from the bones, or tear apart if using breasts.
9. Assemble your salad. Fluff up the leaves in the middle of your crockery to look light and airy.
10. Arrange the salad vegetables and ripped roast chicken in the crevices of the leaves.
11. Top with hazelnuts, dressing, fresh herbs and garnish of choice.

TOPPINGS

- Handful of hazelnuts, lightly toasted and roughly chopped
- Up to 50g chopped fresh herbs: parsley, chives, dill (optional), mint (optional)
- Up to 50g broccoli or alfalfa sprouts (optional)
- 1 fresh chilli, sliced and deseeded (optional)
- 2 tbsp mixed seeds (optional)

⇄ SWAPS

Nut-free: omit the hazelnuts

RECIPE BY CATHERINE SHARMAN

Experienced qualified nutritionist and passionate chef with extensive knowledge and experience of developing nutritionally-functional meals for everyone.

 www.apresfood.com   ApresFoodCo   @apresfoodco

I've used the term 'superfood' for this salad to describe the amazing nutritional benefits of eating plenty of different brightly coloured plant foods. The combination of these plant pigments helps to protect your body at a cellular level – something I think is pretty super from a salad.

SUPERFOOD SALAD

Katie says: *"This salad is a favourite recommendation of mine because this 'assembly' style cooking is quick and can be done at work, when you're in a rush, or even one-handed if you're holding a baby.*

"Quick and healthy food doesn't have to be complicated, and the beetroots, tomatoes and bell peppers are packed full of folate, vitamin C and potassium, whilst the salad greens are some of the best choices for antioxidants, iron and B vitamins. Eating healthy fats with fruits and vegetables can be helpful because some vitamins are only fat-soluble, meaning we need fat to be able to absorb them. Don't skip your dressing, it's essential to get the most nutritional benefit out of your food!"

SERVES	TIME	PLANTS
2-4	10 mins	8

METHOD

1. Microwave the grains according to the packet instructions, usually 2 minutes.
2. Meanwhile, add the salad leaves to a plate. Then add the cherry tomatoes, bell pepper and beetroot.
3. Sprinkle goat's cheese over the salad. Add the smoked mackerel fillet.
4. Once the grains have cooked, add enough to fill ¼ of each plate.
5. Put the salad dressing ingredients into an empty jar or container and shake until combined.
6. Pour the dressing over the salad and sprinkle the pumpkin seeds on top.

⇄ SWAPS

Vegetarian: omit the mackerel or substitute it for another protein, such as tinned (and drained) chickpeas
Vegan and dairy-free: swap the goat's cheese with a dairy-free alternative. For vegan, use the vegetarian swap too

If you don't like mackerel but eat meat, substitute it for cooked chicken
Any grain/rice packets can be substituted, although wholegrains are recommended; any colour bell pepper or tomato variety would work

INGREDIENTS

- 1 x 200g-250g packet of microwave grains, e.g. quinoa or wholegrain rice
- 2 x 80g packets rocket, watercress and spinach salad mix (or 50g of each)
- 10-12 cherry tomatoes, chopped
- 1 orange or yellow bell pepper, roughly chopped
- 2 beetroots, ready-cooked and roughly chopped
- 4 tbsp soft goat's cheese, in small chunks
- 2 smoked mackerel fillets
- 2 tbsp pumpkin seeds

For the salad dressing

- 6 tbsp extra virgin olive oil
- 2 tbsp white wine vinegar
- 2 tsp Dijon mustard
- Salt and pepper to taste

RECIPE BY KATIE SHORE

Katie is a registered nutritional therapist specialising in fertility, pregnancy and postnatal health. She supports women to be as healthy as possible so that they can have a baby, enjoy their pregnancy or recover from birth. She lives in Bedfordshire with her husband and son.

 www.katieshore.co.uk   @katie_intuitivewellbeing

RAINBOW BUDDHA BOWL

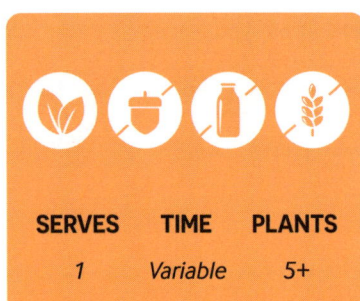

SERVES	**TIME**	**PLANTS**
1	*Variable*	*5+*

PROTEIN

- Meat or poultry, oven-roasted or pan-fried, cubed
- Tofu, pan-fried and cubed
- Fish, baked
- Seafood, e.g. prawns, scallops
- Boiled egg, quartered
- Cheese, e.g. pan-fried halloumi or paneer, feta, cheddar, cottage cheese
- Any cooked bean or pulse

OPTIONAL EXTRAS

- 2 tsp nuts or seeds
- Any spice or herb to taste

Kirstie says: *"A rainbow Buddha bowl is a bowl made up of a protein and a rainbow of colour. From the lists below, choose approximately 150g of a protein of choice and then approximately 50g of one food from each of the different colours listed. Add extras as desired. Top with a dressing and enjoy!"*

DRESSINGS

Tahini dressing

- *50g tahini*
- *20ml lemon juice*
- *50ml water (replace with yoghurt for creamy tahini dressing)*
- *1 garlic clove, crushed*
- *1 tsp honey*
- *Salt and pepper to taste*

Peanut dressing

- *50g smooth peanut butter*
- *2 tsp soy sauce*
- *1 tsp sweet chilli sauce*
- *2 tsp lime juice*
- *2 tsp water to thin out (adjust according to preference)*

Yoghurt and mint dressing

- *50g yoghurt*
- *1 tsp lemon juice*
- *2 tsp mint, finely chopped*

French dressing

- *50ml olive oil*
- *25ml balsamic vinegar*
- *¼ tsp Dijon mustard*
- *½ tsp sugar*
- *Salt and pepper to taste*

Honey mustard dressing

- *50ml olive oil*
- *1 tsp Dijon mustard*
- *1 tsp honey*
- *1 tsp lemon juice*
- *Salt and pepper to taste*

Soy and sesame dressing

- *20ml olive oil*
- *20ml sesame oil*
- *20ml soy sauce*
- *1 tsp lime juice*
- *1 tsp honey*
- *Pinch of chilli flakes*

RECIPE BY DR KIRSTIE LAWTON

Kirstie has been a paediatric nutritionist for 24 years and works predominantly with brain-related health conditions, as well as gut health and immune health-related concerns. She also has a special interest in adults with neurodegenerative conditions such as Parkinson's disease, Huntingdon's disease and motor neurone disease (MND).

 www.younutritionclinic.com   www.nutritionandthebrain.com   @drkirstielawton   @nutritionandthebrain

PURPLE

- Red cabbage, chopped; raw, pickled or sautéed
- Purple carrots, raw or oven-roasted batons
- Aubergine, oven-roasted chunks
- Purple potatoes, boiled chunks or roasted wedges
- Purple cauliflower, in florets, oven-roasted
- Purple kale, roughly chopped and raw, steamed or pan-fried
- Figs, raw or oven-roasted
- Black olives
- Blackberries
- Blueberries
- Prunes
- Raisins

RED

- Beetroot, chopped and roasted, pickled, or grated raw
- Red peppers, chopped, oven-roasted or raw
- Red onion, chopped, oven-roasted or raw
- Tomatoes, oven-roasted or raw
- Red grapes, halved
- Pomegranate seeds
- Berries, dried or fresh
- Fresh watermelon, cubed

ORANGE YELLOW

- Orange or yellow pepper, chopped, oven-roasted or raw
- Corn, cold or warm kernels, or griddled on the cob
- Squash, cubed and oven-roasted
- Apple or pear, grated raw
- Pineapple, in chunks, grilled or raw
- Carrot, grated raw or roasted chunks
- Pumpkin, roasted chunks
- Sweet potato, roasted chunks
- Apricot or mango, dry pieces or fresh cubes

BEIGE

- Any boiled grain, e.g. brown rice, buckwheat, wholegrain couscous, wholegrain pasta, lentil pasta, chickpea pasta, quinoa, barley, rye, spelt
- White potato, boiled chunks or roasted wedges
- Cauliflower, in florets, roasted
- Chickpeas, cooked
- Falafels
- Hummus
- Onion, chopped raw or oven-roasted chunks
- Mushrooms, baked or pan-fried
- Sauerkraut

GREEN

- Asparagus, steamed or sautéed
- Avocado, sliced
- Raw bean sprouts or other sprouted vegetables
- Green pepper, chopped, oven-roasted or raw
- Spring onion, chopped
- Broccoli, in florets, raw or steamed (or any green cruciferous vegetable)
- Collard greens, raw or pan-fried, e.g. kale or spinach
- Salad leaves, e.g. rocket
- Edamame
- Celery, chopped
- Green olives
- Peas, raw or steamed, e.g. garden peas, mange tout or snap peas
- Courgette, chopped and oven-roasted

Soy and sesame chicken bowl

Persian feta bowl

RAINBOW BUDDHA BOWL SUGGESTED COMBINATIONS

SOY AND SESAME CHICKEN BOWL

METHOD

1. Preheat the oven to 180°C/160°C fan/gas mark 4.
2. Drizzle the oil onto a baking tray and add the red pepper, kale and aubergine, keeping them separate but giving them a quick shake to coat them in oil. Season with salt and pepper.
3. Put the vegetables in the oven for 10-15 minutes until the pepper and aubergine are soft and the kale is crispy.
4. Meanwhile, put the cooked quinoa in a bowl, spread into a layer at the bottom. Add the chicken on top, in its own segmented section, followed by the grated carrot next to it.
5. When the vegetables are cooked, arrange them similarly in sections on top of the quinoa, in a round of colour.
6. Add the soy and sesame dressing ingredients to a bowl, jar or small jug, and stir or shake to combine.
7. Pour the dressing over the Buddha bowl and sprinkle with pumpkin seeds to serve.

PERSIAN FETA BOWL

METHOD

1. Preheat the oven to 200°C/180°C fan/gas mark 6.
2. Drizzle the oil onto a baking tray and add the sweet potato, carrots and chickpeas, keeping them separate but giving them a quick shake to coat them in oil. Season with salt and pepper.
3. Put the vegetables in the oven for 30-40 minutes until soft, giving them a shake halfway through.
4. Arrange the feta, lettuce and couscous in sections in a bowl, then fill the rest with the vegetables when cooked.
5. Sprinkle with pomegranate seeds, flaked almonds and parsley.
6. Add the yoghurt and mint dressing ingredients to a bowl, jar or small jug, and stir to combine, before pouring over the Buddha bowl.

INGREDIENTS

Soy and sesame chicken bowl

- 1 tsp olive or sesame oil
- 50g red pepper, roughly chopped
- 50g kale, roughly chopped
- 50g aubergine, chopped
- Salt and pepper to taste
- 50g cooked quinoa
- 150g chicken breast, pre-cooked and cut into pieces
- 50g carrot, peeled and grated
- 2 tsp pumpkin seeds
- Ingredients for soy and sesame dressing (page 74)

Persian feta bowl

- 1 tsp olive oil
- 50g sweet potato, peeled and chopped into chunks
- 50g purple carrots, peeled and chopped into thick batons
- 60g tinned chickpeas, drained and rinsed
- Salt and pepper to taste
- 90g feta cheese, crumbled
- 50g lettuce leaves, washed and roughly chopped
- 50g cooked couscous
- 50g pomegranate seeds
- 2 tsp flaked almonds
- 2 tsp fresh parsley, chopped
- Ingredients for yoghurt and mint dressing (page 74)

Mains

Lamb is a highly-nutritious source of protein, as well as B vitamins including niacin (B3), pantothenic acid (B5), pyridoxine (B6), vitamin B12, iron, selenium and zinc, and other nutrients. Where possible, opt for grass-pastured lamb, as this has a higher nutrient profile.

SPANISH LAMB

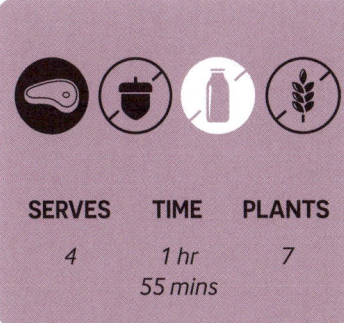

Kirstie says: *"This recipe reminds me of my wonderful years as a charter chef on the trimaran Promenade in the British Virgin Islands, with Cordon Bleu-trained chef Fiona Dugdale, who taught me everything I know about flavours and cooking. This was one of our signature dishes and I've used it at many dinner parties since. The recipe is very adaptable and you can omit or add more of most of the sauce ingredients based on taste preference and allergens.*

"This Spanish lamb dish brings so many nutrients onto one plate, particularly if the recommended sides are also added, providing a rainbow of polyphenols with antioxidant, anti-inflammatory, gut- and liver-supporting, and neuroprotective qualities."

SERVES	TIME	PLANTS
4	1 hr 55 mins	7

METHOD

1. Preheat the oven to 200°C/180°C fan/gas mark 6.
2. In a large roasting pan, heat the oil and butter and then add the onions. Cook for about 10-15 minutes until tender and add the mushrooms; brown slightly for about 10 minutes.
3. Remove the rosemary from the stem and add this and the paprika to the roasting pan. Add in the tomato paste, olives, garlic, stock and red wine, and season to taste. Stir.
4. Add the leg of lamb to the roasting dish and spoon the mixture over. Cover with baking foil and bake on a medium heat for approximately 1 hour 20 minutes, or according to the package instructions (larger pieces of meat will need a longer cooking time) — until the lamb is cooked medium rare.

Serving suggestion: serve with cauliflower cheese (dairy-free if needed), spicy red cabbage and potatoes roasted in olive oil for a delicious, decadent feast.

⇆ SWAPS

Dairy-free: replace the butter with additional olive oil
Lamb alternative: the sauce could also be used for steak/beef

INGREDIENTS

- 20g (approx. 1½ tbsp) olive oil
- 10g butter
- 2 medium onions, sliced
- 150g button mushrooms, trimmed, wiped and sliced
- 1 stem of fresh rosemary
- 20g paprika
- 1 tube of tomato paste
- 20 green olives
- 2 garlic cloves, crushed
- 200ml gluten-free beef stock
- 100ml red wine
- Salt and pepper to season
- 1 leg of lamb

RECIPE BY DR KIRSTIE LAWTON

Kirstie has been a paediatric nutritionist for 24 years and works predominantly with brain-related health conditions, as well as gut health and immune health-related concerns. She also has a special interest in adults with neurodegenerative conditions such as Parkinson's disease, Huntingdon's disease and motor neurone disease (MND).

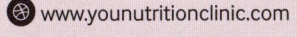 www.younutritionclinic.com 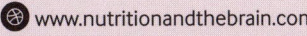 www.nutritionandthebrain.com 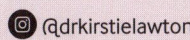 @drkirstielawton 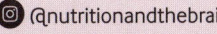 @nutritionandthebrain

CURRIED LAMB MINCE

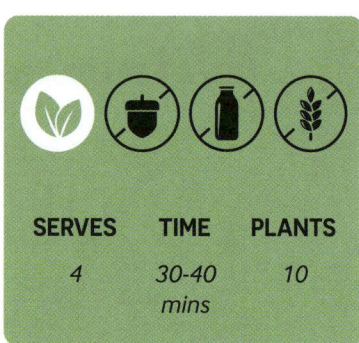

SERVES 4

TIME 30-40 mins

PLANTS 10

INGREDIENTS

- 1 tbsp olive oil
- 2 tbsp nigella seeds
- 8 garlic cloves, finely chopped
- 500g lamb mince
- 1 medium onion, finely diced
- 1 tbsp ground turmeric
- 1 tsp chilli powder
- Himalayan or sea salt and black pepper to taste
- 1 x 400g tin chopped tomatoes
- 1 tbsp ground coriander
- 1 tbsp ground cumin
- 2 tbsp fresh root ginger, peeled and grated
- 25g fresh coriander, chopped
- 2 plum tomatoes, finely chopped
- 1 green chilli, finely chopped

Melissa says: *"I particularly like this recipe because it's so easy to make. It is very adaptable according to whether you eat meat or not, and you can make double the quantity and freeze it for another day. It also tastes fabulous and contains a bunch of immune-supportive spices!"*

METHOD

1. Pour the olive oil into a deep saucepan, add the nigella seeds and garlic and cook over a low-medium heat until the garlic is a golden-brown colour, stirring frequently. This should take no more than 2-3 minutes.
2. Into the saucepan add the lamb, onion, turmeric, chilli powder, salt and pepper. Mix well and cook for about 5 minutes, or until the lamb is sealed all over, stirring frequently.
3. Pour the tinned tomatoes into the meat and spice mixture and stir through. Reduce to a low simmer and cook, covered, for 20-30 minutes, stirring occasionally.
4. Mix in the ground coriander, ground cumin, ginger, fresh chopped coriander, chopped plum tomatoes and green chilli. Continue to cook uncovered for 5 minutes, stirring frequently.

Serving suggestion: serve with basmati rice or cauliflower rice, mango chutney, fried okra or steamed broccoli. It also goes well with homemade gluten-free flatbreads for a weekend treat.

⇆ SWAPS

Pescetarian, vegetarian or vegan: swap the lamb mince with firm white fish, salmon, chickpeas or your favourite beans. Make the sauce, then add your protein, so it doesn't overcook.

RECIPE BY MELISSA SMITH

Melissa graduated from the Institute for Optimum Nutrition (ION) in 2014 with the aim of using nutritional therapy to get to the root of health issues and help people regain their balance, equilibrium and vigour. In 2016, she joined the team at the natural health not-for-profit, Alliance for Natural Health International (www.anhinternational.org), where she has been able to put her nutritional therapy experience to good use supporting the ANH's work and its supporters ever since.

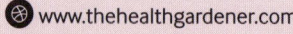 www.thehealthgardener.com　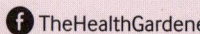 TheHealthGardener　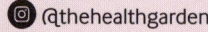 @thehealthgardener

For more plant goodness, you can also add in some sliced leeks, grated carrot or courgette, or sliced peppers or mushrooms — but you might need an extra splash of water or stock as well.

A slow cooker cooks food at a lower temperature, which helps to preserve some of the vitamins and minerals in the food.

SLOW COOKER SAUSAGE AND BEAN HOT POT

Catherine says: *"I love a slow cooker recipe – just put it on and let it work its magic! This recipe is great because it's packed with fibre-rich veggies and pulses.*

"Beans are a common food of some of the world's longest living people, and provide an excellent source of fibre for your friendly gut bugs."

SERVES	TIME	PLANTS
4-6	2-6 hr	11

METHOD

1. Put the sausages under the grill and cook until brown on both sides (about 10-15 minutes, turning occasionally).
2. Meanwhile, heat the olive oil in a small frying pan and sauté the celery and onion for 5 minutes, until translucent. Add the garlic and stir for another minute. Remove from the heat and add the vegetables to the slow cooker.
3. Put all the other ingredients into the slow cooker, except for the broccoli, and stir well.
4. Once browned, arrange the sausages in the slow cooker and cook on low heat for 5-6 hours, or high heat for 2-3 hours.
5. For the last 15 minutes, check the seasoning and add extra salt or pepper if needed. Stir and then lay the broccoli on top to cook.

Serving suggestion: serve with mashed sweet potatoes or sweet potato wedges or simply enjoy on its own.

INGREDIENTS

- 10-12 good quality sausages
- 1 tbsp olive oil
- 3 sticks of celery, chopped
- 1 red onion, finely chopped
- 2 garlic cloves, crushed
- 3 carrots, washed or peeled and chopped
- ⅓ red cabbage, finely chopped
- 1 x 400g tin chickpeas, drained and rinsed
- 1 x 400g tin kidney beans, drained and rinsed
- 6 chestnut mushrooms, halved
- 1 bottle passata (690g bottle)
- 350ml water
- 1 stock cube (beef or vegetable)
- 1 tsp smoked paprika
- Pinch of salt and pepper to taste
- Small head of broccoli, chopped into florets

⇄ SWAPS

Vegan: leave out the sausages and add some extra beans or tofu
Gluten-free: use gluten-free sausages and stock cube
Spicier: add a pinch of cayenne or some chilli flakes

RECIPE BY CATHERINE JEANS

Catherine is a functional nutritional therapist, supporting children and adults of all ages with digestive health, hormone balance, weight management, stress relief and neurodiversity. Her ethos is to empower clients towards a lifetime of good health, using simple, everyday food and lifestyle changes.

 www.thefamilynutritionexpert.com   familynutritionexpert   @catherine_jeans

MAKES	TIME	PLANTS
12 meatballs	35 mins	0

INGREDIENTS

- 200g pork liver, roughly chopped
- 750g beef mince
- 50g 100% beef suet* (optional)
- 2 tsp celtic salt
- 1 tbsp pork lard or beef dripping, for cooking

beef suet is the hardened fat from a cow which you can purchase from online from a butcher or meat specialist; be careful not to buy suet with any additives like wheat flour

PORK LIVER AND BEEF MEATBALLS

Moira says: *"This recipe is a great choice if you are following a carnivore diet. Many people struggle to know how best to incorporate organ meat into their diet and this is a very tasty way to do it. It is also very nutrient dense and so is a great recipe for anyone who wants to use a food first approach without supplements."*

METHOD

1. Place all the ingredients (except the lard/dripping) in a food processor and blitz until well mixed.
2. Put 1 tbsp of the lard or dripping in a pan on a medium-high heat. Once the fat is hot, form the meat mixture into small meatballs with your hands, flatten slightly and place into the pan.
3. Once all the meatballs are in the pan, leave them for a few minutes until browned and turn over and repeat. After this, put a lid on to stop the fat splattering, turn the heat down to medium and leave until they are cooked through, turning occasionally. (Be careful not to get burned as lard and dripping do tend to spit more.)

Serving suggestion: if following a carnivore diet, serve with the remaining fat poured over the meatballs and a little pork crackling on the side, or with some bone marrow fat for some extra vitamin C. If not following a carnivore diet, serve with a side dish of vegetables such as broccoli and cauliflower (for a ketogenic diet) or roasted turnip and celeriac chips (if you want to stay low with your carbohydrate intake).

⇆ **SWAPS**

Lower fat: leave out the suet
Added veg: add diced, sautéed onion or mushrooms
Flavour: add extra herbs and spices

RECIPE BY MOIRA NEWISS

Moira uses a variety of approaches in her work, all of which have a food first focus, including low carbohydrate, ketogenic and carnivore diets. She has personal experience of making a full recovery from chronic fatigue and anxiety, reversing insulin resistance and putting Hashimoto's thyroiditis into remission. Moira lives in Scotland with her husband, two teenage children and five chickens where she can indulge in her passion for climbing the mountains and bikepacking fuelled on fat as a fuel.

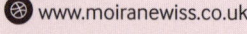 www.moiranewiss.co.uk 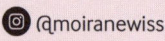 @moiranewiss 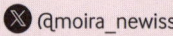 @moira_newiss 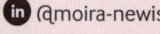 @moira-newiss

> This is my favourite way to eat liver. I'm not a big fan of the taste and texture of liver but ground up in a meatball it is delicious (to be honest I don't notice it!). Liver is a powerhouse of nutrition packed with protein and vitamins such as B12, B2, B9 (folate), iron, copper and choline. Vitamin B12 is only found in animal foods and B9 is not as common in animal foods but liver is a great source of it.

Button, chestnut, portobello, crimini, shiitake, maitake: there are many different types of edible mushroom available in the supermarket or grocery shop. I recommend using a broad variety of mushrooms in your cooking as each mushroom has a different nutritional profile and health benefits. It's easy to use just a couple of each type in a recipe like this one, to support diversity and variety in our food, and therefore in our gut bacteria!

MINCED PORK WITH PEPPERS AND MUSHROOMS

Robyn says: *"This meal is a family favourite as it's the perfect intersection between real, good, family food and food that nourishes your body and gut. It's full of flavour and is warming and comforting. I recommend this to clients because it's easy to make, very nutrient dense and can be pre-made for easy weekday meals."*

METHOD

This can be made on the stove, or in an instant pot or slow cooker.

1. In a bowl, mix the pork mince with the herbs, spices and red wine vinegar, using a spatula to break up the mince. Place to the side.

ON THE STOVE TOP

2. Heat 1 tbsp of olive oil in a large pan over a medium heat and add the onion. Sauté for a few minutes until translucent and then add the garlic, mushrooms and peppers. Gently sauté for a further 10-15 minutes until the mushrooms are moderately cooked and the pepper is soft. Transfer the vegetables to a bowl and set aside.

3. Add the remaining oil to the pan and fry the pork mince until browned – about 7 minutes. Add back the vegetables, salt and passata, turn down the heat and simmer for 30 minutes until everything is cooked thoroughly and fragrant. Wilt in a handful of spinach or other leafy greens at the end of cooking, if desired.

IN AN INSTANT POT

Brown the onion and add to the bowl with the mince, mushrooms, peppers, garlic, salt and passata and stir well. Pressure cook for 10 minutes and then leave for 30 minutes to de-pressure. This can be left on warming for as long as required – the longer this sits the better it gets.

IN A SLOW COOKER

Brown the onion and add to the slow cooker with the mince, mushrooms, peppers, garlic, salt and passata. Stir and cook on low for 6-8 hours.

⇆ **SWAPS**

Vegan: omit the pork and add yellow, green or brown lentils

Serving suggestion: serve with pasta, rice or other cooked veggies, or just eat it from a bowl! Garnish with fresh parsley, if desired.

MAINS

SERVES	TIME	PLANTS
4	1 hr	12+

INGREDIENTS

- 500g pork mince
- ½ tsp dried thyme
- ½ tsp oregano
- ¼ tsp dried rosemary
- 2 tsp dried parsley
- 1 tsp dried basil
- ½ tsp smoked paprika
- Crushed red pepper flakes, to taste
- ½ tsp fennel seeds
- ½ tsp cracked black pepper
- 1 tbsp red wine vinegar
- 2 tbsp olive oil (1 tbsp if using an instant pot or slow cooker)
- 1 large red onion (or ½ red, ½ yellow for more variety), diced
- 2 small garlic cloves, crushed
- 300g mixed mushrooms, chopped
- 4 mixed peppers, sliced
- 1 tsp salt
- 1 x 690g jar passata
- Handful of spinach or leafy greens, shredded (optional)

RECIPE BY ROBYN PUGLIA

Robyn specialises in autoimmune disease, gluten-reactive disorders including coeliac disease, complex cases and unexplained illness. As well as her busy clinical practice, Robyn runs The Autoimmune Academy, is co-founder and director of The Applied Functional Medicine Mentoring Program, and is the VP of Education for the UK and EU for Cyrex Laboratories.

 www.robynpuglia.com   @robynpuglia

SERVES	TIME	PLANTS
2-4	1 hr	6+

INGREDIENTS

- 2 tbsp ghee or butter
- 1-2 grass-fed steaks
- ½ white onion, chopped
- 3-4 garlic cloves, minced
- 3-4 large Swiss chard leaves (or any leafy green), chopped
- 1 leek, sliced
- 10 button mushrooms, sliced
- 250ml bone broth or vegetable broth, or stock
- 60g amaranth or garbanzo bean flour, or all-purpose flour
- 2 tsp smoked paprika
- 3 tbsp Greek yoghurt (or a goat/dairy-free alternative)
- Pinch of salt and ground pepper and/or chilli flakes
- Grated parmesan or nutritional yeast, to serve

SAVOURY STROGANOFF

Kaley says: *"This recipe is easy to make and very adaptable for dietary restrictions. It's a great source of protein, high in prebiotic fibre (leek, garlic and onion) and various nutrients including magnesium. You can use any colourful veggies or spices to add extra colour, flavour and phytonutrients to the meal. This will hopefully be a hit with friends and family!"*

METHOD

1. Heat 1 tbsp of ghee or butter over a medium heat and fry the steak according to your preference. Set aside.
2. Heat the remaining ghee or butter and sauté the onion and garlic for a few minutes. Add the Swiss chard ends and cook for 2 minutes, then add the chard leaves, leeks and mushrooms. Sauté for about 10 minutes, until the vegetables are soft.
3. Meanwhile, heat the broth or stock in a large pan and add the flour and smoked paprika. Let it thicken slightly and then add in the cooked vegetables. Slice the steak and add to the mixture. Mix well.
4. Reduce the heat and gently cook for a few minutes. Add the yoghurt, salt and pepper and/or chilli flakes, and heat for another 4-5 minutes, stirring well.
5. Serve with pasta or rice and a sprinkle of grated parmesan cheese or nutritional yeast.

⇆ SWAPS

Dairy-free: use coconut oil or olive oil instead of ghee or butter, use a dairy-free alternative to Greek yoghurt, and leave out the parmesan cheese or use nutritional yeast instead

Gluten-free: amaranth and garbanzo bean flours are naturally gluten-free, but if you're using all-purpose flour, ensure you choose a gluten-free product. Also, use a gluten-free broth/stock

RECIPE BY KALEY JOHNSON

Kaley began her career as a registered nurse in Canada and practised for 10 years as an advanced critical care nurse. She completed a Master's degree in nursing where her interest in root cause medicine, nutrition and research grew. Now working as a registered nutritional therapist in the UK and Europe, Kaley believes that the philosophical ideals of nursing and functional nutrition have a synergistic potential to help clients identify the root cause of their health concerns.

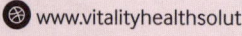 www.vitalityhealthsolutions.org 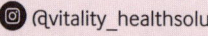 @vitality_healthsolutions   kaley-johnson-84ab522aa

" Magnesium is an amazing mineral that acts as a cofactor in over 600 functions in the body, including maintaining blood sugar balance and converting vitamin D to its active form. It gets depleted during stress. Sources in this meal include mushrooms, green leafy veggies and leeks. "

GNOCCHI BOLOGNESE

Rachel says: *"This recipe is perfect for clients who don't love the taste and texture of vegetables. Loading up on extra vegetables (including any you've got left over in the fridge) is a great way to increase the volume of your meals to keep you fuller for longer, and to get some additional nutrients!"*

SERVES	TIME	PLANTS
4	30-40 mins	6+

METHOD

1. Heat the oil over a medium heat in a large frying pan and then add the onion. Fry gently for about 5 minutes until soft, then add the garlic and cook for another 2 minutes.
2. Add the minced beef and cook until browned, using a spatula to break up the meat.
3. Meanwhile, blitz the peppers, cherry tomatoes and mushrooms with the tinned tomatoes in a blender until the sauce is a smooth consistency. (If you prefer a chunkier sauce, blend for a shorter time or add some/all of the vegetables directly into the pan.) Add the sauce to the mince once the meat has browned.
4. Crumble in the stock cube and then add a pinch of salt and pepper and the chopped basil. If using, add a pinch of chilli flakes and/or a drizzle sriracha, and stir well.
5. Gently simmer on a low-medium heat for about 20 minutes, until the excess liquid has evaporated. Stir occasionally.
6. Stir the gnocchi into the sauce and simmer for about 5 minutes until the gnocchi is soft.
7. To serve, sprinkle over the parmesan and garnish with extra basil leaves, if desired.

⇆ SWAPS

Vegan: swap the minced beef for lentils and/or chickpeas, and use the dairy-free options
Dairy-free: leave out the parmesan or use a dairy-free alternative
Gluten-free: use gluten-free gnocchi and stock cube

INGREDIENTS

- 1 tbsp olive oil
- 1 onion, diced
- 1 garlic clove, minced
- 500g minced beef
- 2 peppers (of any colour), chopped
- 100g cherry tomatoes, chopped
- 100g mushrooms, chopped
- 1 x 400g tin chopped tomatoes
- 1 vegetable stock cube
- Pinch of salt and pepper to taste
- 5-6 leaves basil, chopped, plus a couple of extra leaves to garnish
- Pinch of chilli flakes or drizzle of sriracha (optional)
- 500g gnocchi
- 1-2 tsp grated parmesan (optional)

RECIPE BY RACHEL REES

Rachel is a registered nutritional therapist who is passionate about educating and empowering clients to achieve optimal health through the power of nutrition. She believes that exploring new recipes and experimenting with high-quality ingredients is not only a rewarding process but allows us to appreciate the nutritional value of food.

 www.rachelreesnutrition.com   @rachelreesnutrition

SERVES	TIME	PLANTS
4-6	1 hr 15 - 1 hr 50 mins	8+

INGREDIENTS

- 2 large aubergines, cut into approx. 5cm pieces
- 3 large red onions, peeled and cut into wedges
- 2 courgettes, cut into chunks
- 4 mixed peppers, deseeded and chopped
- 400g cherry/plum tomatoes
- 8 garlic cloves, peeled
- 2 x 400g tins butter beans or chickpeas, drained (optional)
- 4 tbsp sherry vinegar
- 1 tbsp Dijon mustard
- 2 tbsp tomato purée
- 6 sprigs fresh thyme or oregano, or 2-3 tsp dried
- 2 tbsp smoked paprika
- Chilli flakes (optional)
- 80ml olive oil
- Pinch of salt and pepper
- 1 whole or spatchcocked chicken, or 8 chicken thighs

MEDITERRANEAN CHICKEN AND VEGETABLE TRAYBAKE

May says: *"This is my favourite lower-carb take on a Sunday roast: lots more plants and colour but still comforting and filling. It's super easy to prepare, and all done in one tray. Take the tray straight from the oven to the table. It's great served with a fresh green salad and homemade garlic lemon mayo. If you make it on Sunday, leftovers are great eaten for lunch or added to salads throughout the week."*

METHOD

1. Preheat the oven to 200°C/180°C fan/gas mark 6.
2. Place the vegetables, garlic and butter beans or chickpeas (if using) into an extra large baking dish, or two smaller ones.
3. In a bowl, combine the vinegar, mustard, tomato purée, herbs, spices, olive oil, salt and pepper. Mix well.
4. Pour most of the mixture over the vegetables, leaving a small amount to rub into the chicken. Mix thoroughly to ensure the vegetables are evenly coated.
5. If spatchcocking the chicken, use a large sharp knife to cut out the backbone, so you can open it out flat. Sit the chicken skin side up on top of the vegetables. If using chicken thighs, arrange skin side up on top of the vegetables. Rub the remaining olive oil/paprika/herb mixture into the chicken.
6. Roast the chicken and vegetables for approximately 90 minutes for a whole chicken (or according to package instructions), 60 minutes for spatchcock chicken, or 45-50 minutes for thighs, stirring the vegetables midway through. Check the chicken is cooked by inserting the tip of a knife into the thickest part of the thighs: if the juices run clear, the chicken is ready.

⇆ **SWAPS**

Vegan/vegetarian/pescetarian: leave out the chicken to make it vegan, or serve topped with feta to make it vegetarian. It would also work great with white fish like cod, just adjust the cooking time and add the fish 10-15 minutes before serving

RECIPE BY MAY KNIGHT

May is a registered nutritional therapist and type 1 diabetic. She works closely with clients to address a variety of health concerns, with a special interest in blood sugar regulation and digestive health. Her approach to working 1:1 involves delving into the root cause of health issues, rather than simply focusing on symptoms. May is also passionate about developing recipes that promote health and wellbeing, to support clients in reaching their health goals.

 www.mayknightnutrition.com 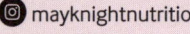 mayknightnutrition

“ Many takeaways are made for maximum taste and minimum cost, which means they often contain added sugar, salt, artificial flavours and flavour enhancers. I'm not against the occasional takeaway – good nutrition is about healthy balance – but this recipe gives you the feel good vibe of nourishing your body as well as your tastebuds. ”

CHICKEN AND SWEET POTATO CURRY

Catherine says: *"This is a family favourite with my own kids and grown-up friends. It's perfect for a Friday night 'fakeaway' with all the flavours but none of the nasties, and is just jam-packed with goodness. It's a slow cooked recipe that can be left alone to cook itself and the timings are very flexible. The longer you leave it, the more the sweet potato melts in to make the sauce. It also freezes well, hence the six portions — perfect for a gathering or to pop some in the freezer for a fast reheat meal in the week."*

SERVES	TIME	PLANTS
6	1 hr 20 mins - 3 hr 20 mins	9+

METHOD

1. Preheat the oven to 170°C/150°C fan/gas mark 3.
2. Heat the coconut oil in a large ovenproof casserole dish and fry the onion on a low heat for 2 minutes, stirring so it doesn't burn. Add the garlic, ginger, turmeric and korma powder and cook for a further 1-2 minutes, stirring to ensure it doesn't stick.
3. Increase the heat to medium and add the chicken. Cook for 3-4 minutes, stirring and turning the pieces until they are white.
4. Add the sweet potato, peppers, chicken stock and coconut milk. Cover the dish with a lid and bring to the boil.
5. Stir well, then transfer the whole dish to the oven to cook slowly for 1-3 hours, checking and stirring occasionally and topping up with a little water if the sauce is getting too thick. This will happen if you leave it cooking for more than an hour, but the flavours are even more delicious if you do cook it a little longer.
6. Remove from the oven when the sauce is fairly thick and the chicken is well cooked and falling apart. Stir in the ground almonds, if using.
7. Sprinkle over the fresh coriander and serve with rice or naan and a veggie side dish.

⇆ SWAPS

Vegan: swap the chicken for chickpeas or fried tofu, added 30 minutes before serving, and swap the chicken stock for vegetable stock
Nut-free: omit the ground almonds

INGREDIENTS

- 1 tbsp coconut oil
- 1 large onion, diced
- 2 garlic cloves, crushed
- 1 heaped tbsp fresh ginger, grated
- 1-2 tsp turmeric powder or fresh grated turmeric
- 2 tbsp korma powder
- 600g chicken, diced into large chunks
- 2 medium sweet potatoes, diced into 2cm chunks
- 2 red peppers, deseeded and diced
- 300-500ml gluten-free chicken stock
- 1 x 400ml tin coconut milk
- 50g ground almonds (optional)
- Handful of chopped fresh coriander, to serve

RECIPE BY CATHERINE POHL

Catherine is a nutritional therapist and health coach based in the icy north of Sweden where she also runs nature-based and wild food retreats. She is passionate about helping her clients with food, lifestyle and mindset strategies to live their very best lives.

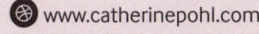 www.catherinepohl.com 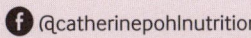 @catherinepohlnutrition 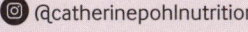 @catherinepohlnutrition

CHICKEN PICCATA

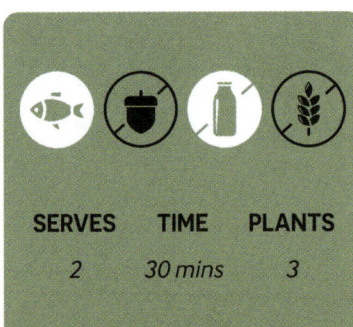

SERVES | **TIME** | **PLANTS**
2 | 30 mins | 3

INGREDIENTS

- 2 large chicken breasts
- 100g ghee or coconut oil
- Zest and juice of 2 lemons
- 50g capers
- Handful of fresh parsley, roughly chopped

VJ says: *"I have a lot of clients asking me for simple recipes with five ingredients or less, and this is one of my favourite recommendations (and dishes to eat myself). It not only contains a superior serving of good-quality protein in the chicken but the capers, lemon and parsley provide an abundance of antioxidants such as quercetin in capers, vitamin C in lemon and vitamin A in parsley."*

METHOD

1. Put the chicken breasts between two pieces of kitchen roll and pound with a rolling pin until flattened.
2. In a large frying pan, add a quarter of the ghee or coconut oil (25g) and sauté the chicken breasts in the pan until just cooked through. Transfer the chicken onto a plate and cover.
3. Add the remaining ghee or coconut oil to the pan and combine with half the lemon zest, and the lemon juice and capers, and heat for 2 minutes.
4. Add the chicken back to the pan and cook with the other ingredients for a couple of minutes, and then add the parsley.
5. Spoon the sauce over the chicken and then serve on two plates. Garnish with the remaining lemon zest.

Serving suggestion: optionally serve with sautéed garlicky spinach, and lemon and garlic cauliflower rice, using some of the lemon juice and zest.

⇆ **SWAPS**

Pescetarian: replace the chicken with cod
Dairy-free: use coconut oil instead of ghee

RECIPE BY VICTORIA (VJ) HAMILTON

VJ founded The Autoimmunity Nutritionist Clinic and is a registered nutritionist and autoimmune disease expert focusing on autoimmune skin conditions, alopecia, chronic fatigue, joint issues and gut health. VJ has a BSc in Immunology, which she uses in her practice, using only evidence-based nutritional therapies to support her clients.

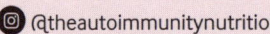 theautoimmunitynutritionist.com @theautoimmunitynutritionist

Olives *(Olea europaea)* are related to mango, cherry and peaches. Use extra virgin olive oil on a daily basis; research suggests the oleic acid (omega-9) can reduce the risk of heart disease and has anti-inflammatory properties. In *Gulliver's Travels*, Gulliver spent eight years trying to extract sunbeams from cucumbers, but I always thought that olives were the food which, when eaten, fill us with warm sunshine.

ALGERIAN CHICKEN WITH LEMON AND OLIVES

Dian says: *"We used to cook this dish with my friend's family when we were on holiday in Algiers. It is very tasty and is full of Mediterranean flavours. We have very happy memories of the wonderful heat, walks through the Casbah and markets with aromas of spices, shops full of hammered silverware, music in the background, sitting around talking with the family in the garden under the fig trees during long evening meals under the stars."*

SERVES	TIME	PLANTS
2	1 hr 15 mins	8

METHOD

1. Heat the oil over a medium heat and then add the chicken, spices and garlic. Sauté for 15 minutes, turning the chicken occasionally.
2. Once cooked, set the chicken to one side, and add the butter to the remaining jus in the pan. Sauté the onions with the salt and pepper until softened – about 5 minutes.
3. Return the chicken to the pan with the water, chopped parsley, stock powder/cube and lemon quarters, and simmer for 30 minutes. Stir regularly and don't let it dry out.
4. Add the olives and simmer for a further 5-10 minutes.

Serving suggestion: serve with boiled white basmati rice (cooked with a pinch of salt, 4 cloves and 4 peppercorns – removed before serving) and either a crisp green watercress and rocket salad with a lemon and olive oil dressing, or boiled peas and sliced green beans.

⇆ SWAPS

Dairy-free: swap the butter with a non-dairy alternative or olive oil
Without olives: if you don't like olives, leave them out or use finely-diced green peppers instead

INGREDIENTS

- 1 tbsp extra virgin olive oil
- 2 chicken breasts, cut into pieces
- ¼ tsp ground ginger
- ¼ tsp cumin
- ¼ tsp turmeric
- 1 small garlic clove, finely chopped
- 2 medium onions, finely chopped
- 25g butter
- ¼ tsp sea salt
- Pinch of pepper
- 300ml water (extra as needed)
- 1 tbsp fresh parsley, chopped
- 1 tsp gluten-free vegetable stock powder or 1 vegetable stock cube
- 1 non-waxed lemon, quartered and pips removed
- 8 green olives

RECIPE BY DIAN SHEPPERSON MILLS

Dian's research interests include endometriosis, sub-fertility, endocrine disorders, coeliac disease and the gut microbiome. She has published several papers and abstracts in *Fertility and Sterility*, written book chapters and lectured to scientific associations around the world. Her books are: *Endometriosis: A Key to Healing and Fertility Through Nutrition* (Thorsons); *Making Babies: The Nutrition Recipe* (The Endometriosis and Fertility Clinic); and a chapter in *Integrated Approaches to Infertility, IVF and Recurrent Miscarriages: A Handbook* (Singing Dragon).

 www.endometriosis.co.uk 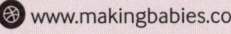 www.makingbabies.com

SERVES	TIME	PLANTS
2	20 mins	12+

INGREDIENTS

- 2 tbsp extra virgin olive oil
- 250g chicken breast fillets, cut into bitesize pieces
- 4 spring onions, finely sliced
- 2 garlic cloves, crushed
- 1 thumb-sized piece ginger, finely grated
- 1 red chilli, finely chopped
- 1 medium courgette, spiralised,
- 1 carrot, julienned or grated
- 6 sprigs of tenderstem broccoli, chopped into florets
- ½ red pepper, thinly sliced
- ½ yellow pepper, thinly sliced
- ¼ red cabbage, finely shredded or grated
- ½ small bunch fresh coriander leaves, chopped, to serve

For the peanut butter sauce

- Juice of 1 lime
- 6 tbsp tamari
- 6 tbsp smooth peanut butter
- Pinch of chilli flakes (optional)

RAINBOW PAD THAI

Charlotte says: *"This recipe is an easy way to bring more veg to your table. It's super quick, fuss-free and beyond delicious — the perfect meal for busy weeknights. Tamari is gluten-free soy sauce and uses fewer ingredients, and I recommend it even if you're not following a gluten-free diet.*

"If you have a food processor, make life easier by grating all your vegetables together. It doesn't need to look pretty — just taste good!"

METHOD

1. To make the sauce, place the lime juice, tamari, peanut butter and chilli flakes (if using) in a small bowl or food processor and whisk or blitz until smooth. Add a little water to thin, if needed. Set aside.
2. Heat 1 tbsp of the oil in a small frying pan and stir-fry the chicken until cooked through.
3. Meanwhile, heat the remaining olive oil in a large frying pan or wok over a medium-high heat. Add the onion, garlic, ginger and chilli and stir-fry for 1 minute, or until fragrant; stir continuously to avoid burning.
4. Add the vegetables to the large frying pan and stir-fry for 5 minutes or until the broccoli turns vibrant green. Add the sauce and cooked chicken, mix to combine and warm through for about 1 minute.
5. Divide between serving bowls and sprinkle with coriander to serve.

⇆ **SWAPS**

Vegan: omit the chicken or swap for tofu
Nut-free: swap the peanut butter for light tahini
No spiraliser: finely slice or grate the courgette instead

RECIPE BY CHARLOTTE GRAND

Charlotte is a registered nutritional therapist, author of *The Fertility Kitchen* cookbook and creator of the popular Instagram channels @thefertilitykitchen and @themenopausekitchen where she shares her balanced approach and everyday recipes. She is passionate about helping women transform their health at every life stage.

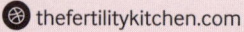 thefertilitykitchen.com 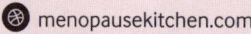 menopausekitchen.com 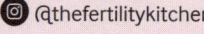 @thefertilitykitchen 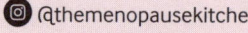 @themenopausekitchen

The recipe works best with a smooth, thick, well-blended peanut butter. Avoid using peanut butter that has separated. You can also use almond butter or tahini.

By using mackerel instead of the traditional haddock, creamed up at the end with a tablespoon of tahini, and a smaller serving of wholegrain bulgur or quinoa instead of rice, this spicy kedgeree ends up high in fat with a low glycaemic load.

PATRICK'S LOW-CARB KEDGEREE

Patrick says: *"This recipe ticks all the boxes: high in omega-3 and vitamin B12, great for the brain; low GL [glycaemic load] so great for weight control; high in folate and other B vitamins so supports methylation, along with B12 in the mackerel; and high in antioxidants and polyphenols from the spices, black pepper and veg."*

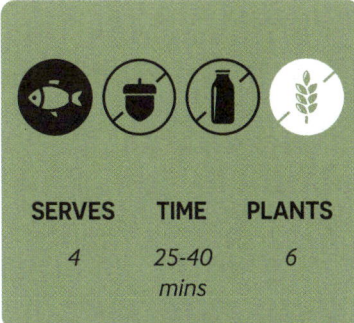

SERVES	TIME	PLANTS
4	25-40 mins	6

METHOD

1. Measure out three times as much water as bulgur, quinoa or brown basmati rice in a pan and bring it to the boil. Add the bulgur, quinoa or rice and simmer on a low heat for 8 minutes (bulgur), 13 minutes (quinoa) or 35 minutes (brown rice), then drain any surplus water, if needed.
2. Meanwhile, hard boil the eggs in a pan of boiling water for 6 minutes then cool rapidly under the tap for a minute. Set aside to fully cool before peeling and slicing into quarters.
3. Heat the olive oil in a large saucepan and sweat the garlic and onion for a minute or so before adding the spices. Let them gently cook for a further few minutes, taking care not to let them burn, until the onions are soft and fragrant.
4. Break the smoked mackerel into small pieces and add to the saucepan, stirring them in.
5. Meanwhile, add the petit pois to boiling water and wait until the water is boiling again, then add the broccoli pieces. Once the peas float to the top, remove from the heat, drain, then add to the onion and mackerel.
6. Stir in the cooked grains until evenly coated and then add the hard-boiled eggs.
7. Stir in the tahini to make it creamy and season with plenty of pepper. You won't need any salt thanks to the salty smoked fish and the strength of the spices. Garnish with the parsley.

⇆ SWAPS

Gluten-free: use quinoa or brown rice instead of bulgur wheat
Lowest carb: use quinoa instead of bulgur wheat or brown rice

INGREDIENTS

- 60g wholegrain bulgur wheat, quinoa or brown rice – makes 180g cooked
- 2 eggs
- 2 tbsp mild or medium olive oil (not extra virgin), virgin rapeseed oil or coconut oil
- 1 garlic clove, crushed
- 1 large or 2 small onions, finely chopped
- ½-1 tsp ground smoked paprika or cayenne
- ½-1 tsp ground cumin
- ½-1 tsp ground turmeric
- 2 smoked mackerel fillets (approx. 275g)
- 100g frozen petit pois
- 200g tenderstem broccoli, cut in half
- 1 tbsp tahini
- Black pepper to taste
- 4 tbsp flat leaf parsley, finely chopped

RECIPE BY PATRICK HOLFORD

Patrick is a leading spokesman on nutrition and mental health and founder of both the Food for the Brain Foundation and the Institute for Optimum Nutrition (ION). Originally trained in psychology, Patrick was one of the first promoters of the importance of zinc, essential fats, low-GL diets and homocysteine-lowering B vitamins for mental health and Alzheimer's prevention. Patrick is the author of 46 books, translated into over 30 languages, including *The Optimum Nutrition Bible* and his latest book *Upgrade Your Brain*. Patrick is also in the Orthomolecular Medicine Hall of Fame.

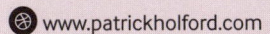 www.patrickholford.com 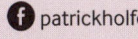 patrickholford ⊙ @patrickholford.uk

SERVES 2-3 **TIME** 25 mins **PLANTS** 6+

INGREDIENTS

- 1 small butternut squash, spiralised
- 1 tbsp extra virgin olive oil
- Salt to taste
- 1-2 tsp oregano
- 2 tsp coconut oil
- 1 red onion, finely chopped
- 3 garlic cloves, minced
- 200g boneless sardines, either fresh or tinned
- Zest and juice of 1 lemon
- Handful of fresh parsley, chopped
- Salad leaves to serve (optional)

LEMONY SARDINES WITH BUTTERNUT SQUASH 'LINGUINI'

VJ says: *"This Italian-inspired dish is packed with flavour and simple to prepare. The sardines' salty and buttery taste is wonderfully complemented with a lemony punch and earthiness of parsley. Sardines are an excellent source of vitamin D, which supports mental health, memory and your ability to think clearly. Sardines also contain docosahexaenoic acid (DHA), a type of omega-3 fat that improves brain function."*

METHOD

1. Preheat the oven to 220°C/200°C fan/gas mark 7.
2. Add the spiralised butternut squash to a baking tray and sprinkle with olive oil. Season with salt and oregano. Put in the oven and bake for 20 minutes.
3. After 10 minutes, put a frying pan on medium heat and add the coconut oil. Add the onions and garlic and lightly fry for 5 minutes.
4. Add the sardines and lemon zest and cook for a further 2 minutes, before adding the parsley and lemon juice to finish.
5. Remove the butternut squash from the oven and serve on two or three plates. Top with the lemony sardines and accompany with salad leaves of your choice, if desired.

⇆ **SWAPS**

Don't have a spiraliser? If you'd still like butternut squash, you can try grating it or making ribbons with a peeler. Alternatively, swap it out for pasta, ditch it for more salad leaves (low-carb option), or just have lemony sardines on toast.

RECIPE BY VICTORIA (VJ) HAMILTON

VJ founded The Autoimmunity Nutritionist Clinic and is a registered nutritionist and autoimmune disease expert focusing on autoimmune skin conditions, alopecia, chronic fatigue, joint issues and gut health. VJ has a BSc in Immunology, which she uses in her practice, using only evidence-based nutritional therapies to support her clients.

 theautoimmunitynutritionist.com   @theautoimmunitynutritionist

" The omega-3 fatty acids in sardines and other oily fish promote an anti-inflammatory response in the body, which may help those with chronic illness and autoimmune disease. Omega-3 fatty acids can also promote higher levels of HDL (high-density lipoprotein) cholesterol, which is often referred to as 'good' cholesterol. "

Always check the full ingredients of soba noodles if there is a gluten allergy. Traditionally, soba noodles would be made only with buckwheat, making them 100% gluten-free; however, some companies add wheat flour to their products.

MISO TROUT WITH SESAME AND ORANGE SOBA NOODLES

Tessa says: *"A lot of people struggle with introducing fish into their diet. Helping clients increase their omegas is rather easy with the delicious miso dressing. An added bonus is that the miso is fermented, so it contains probiotics and other essential vitamins and minerals. The fish skin is packed with extra omega-3, vitamins B and D, and collagen, so give it a try! You might be surprised."*

SERVES	TIME	PLANTS
2-3	45 mins	7

METHOD

1. Boil the noodles according to the packet instructions and drain.
2. Blend the orange and sesame dressing ingredients together, if possible, as the sesame seeds make the dressing slightly creamy. Alternatively, just whisk them together in a bowl.
3. In a separate bowl, mix the miso dressing ingredients with 4 tbsp of the orange dressing, then set aside.
4. Heat 1 tsp oil in a pan, add shallots and greens and stir-fry for 3-5 minutes. This may take longer depending on the vegetable. If using broccoli, for example, it will take longer; add a splash of water to help soften it up.
5. Add the noodles back into the pan, add 4 tbsp orange dressing and toss with the vegetables. Set aside.
6. Meanwhile, wipe or rinse the pan and place it on medium heat. Add 1 tsp oil and once hot, place the trout skin side down, allowing the skin to get crispy.
7. Pan-fry the fish according to the packet instructions, or for up to 4 minutes on each side (8 minutes in total). After about 5 minutes, pour over the miso marinade and allow the fish to be glazed.
8. Remove the skin if you are not planning to eat it – it should peel off easily.
9. Flip for 10 seconds to cover the trout in glaze and place on the noodles.
10. Scatter fresh coriander over the noodles.

INGREDIENTS

- 200g soba noodles (100% buckwheat if possible)
- 2 tsp oil (coconut/olive)
- 1 shallot or spring onion, chopped
- 160g asparagus, broccoli or any greens in your fridge, chopped
- 350g trout (about 3 fillets)
- Handful of fresh coriander, chopped

For the orange and sesame dressing

- Juice of 1 orange
- 3 tbsp toasted sesame seeds
- 3 tbsp olive oil
- 2 tbsp vinegar (rice/red/white)
- 1 tbsp soy sauce or tamari
- 1 tsp honey or agave (optional)

For the miso dressing

- 1 tsp brown miso paste
- ¼ tsp grated ginger

⇆ SWAPS

Vegan: swap the trout with tofu and omit the honey from the orange dressing, or use agave instead
Gluten-free: use 100% buckwheat noodles or swap for courgette noodles; use tamari not soy sauce in the orange dressing, and use gluten-free miso

RECIPE BY TESSA MERTEN

After working in the food industry for nine years, Tessa truly began experiencing how the body reacted to food and was fascinated at how much control we actually have. Her mission became finding out how to live our best lives, instead of simply existing.

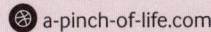 a-pinch-of-life.com @cape.town.nutrition

MEDITERRANEAN FISH BAKE

SERVES 2

TIME 45 mins

PLANTS 8

Kate says: *"This fish bake is based on a recipe idea from Abel and Cole. It is quick and easy to prepare, and its simplicity belies its satisfying deliciousness!*

"Fresh fish, tomatoes and fragrant herbs form the basis of this tasty Mediterranean fish stew. The Mediterranean diet is reputed to be the most studied diet in the world for it's health benefits, based on fresh and, if possible, local ingredients."

INGREDIENTS

- 1 tsp olive oil
- 1 celery stick, finely sliced
- 1 onion, finely chopped
- 1 carrot, finely diced
- 2 garlic cloves, crushed
- Handful of flat leaf parsley, leaves separated from stems, all roughly chopped
- ½ tsp ground coriander
- Salt and pepper to taste
- 1 bay leaf
- 1 x 400g tin chopped tomatoes
- 100ml water
- 1 x 300-375g pack of fish pie mix, or a mix of white fish and salmon, cut into small chunks
- 25g parmesan, finely grated

METHOD

1. Heat the oil in a frying pan on a medium-low heat, and add the chopped celery, onion and carrot. Cook for 8 minutes to soften the vegetables, stirring occasionally.
2. Preheat your grill to high, or oven to 200°C/180°C fan/gas mark 6.
3. Add the garlic, parsley stems and coriander to the vegetables, season with salt and pepper, and stir well to combine. After a minute or two, add the bay leaf, chopped tomatoes and water. Put the lid on and simmer for 16 minutes until the tomato sauce thickens, occasionally lifting the lid to give it a stir.
4. Taste the sauce and add more seasoning if you like. Stir in the (raw) fish pie mix and transfer to an open ovenproof dish. Top with parmesan.
5. Grill or bake for 5-8 minutes until the parmesan is golden and the sauce is bubbling.
6. Once cooked, remove from the oven and leave to rest for just a few minutes, before adding the chopped parsley leaves.

Serving suggestion: serve with a fresh green salad.

⇆ **SWAPS**

Dairy-free: leave out the parmesan

RECIPE BY KATE COOK

Kate graduated from the Institute for Optimum Nutrition (ION) in 2000 and is an international speaker on nutrition and health, and author of eight books – the latest, *Positive Nutrition*, was published in 2018. She is founder of The Nutrition Network, an independent community for the nutritional therapy industry, founded in 2010.

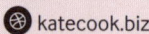 katecook.biz 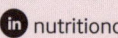 nutritioncoach

"A thermos flask can keep food warm for an easy and cheap lunch, whilst a slow-cooked meal can be ready for you when you get in from work. All of this means less stress around food."

GOAN FISH OR TOFU CURRY

Charlotte says: *"This meal fits into a bit of a fixation of mine — eating from bowls as our ancestors would have done, preferably around a fire! A bowl of curry, soup or stew can be a great comforter in the winter months, on a chilly evening, or just for those times when we feel we need some inner warmth.*

"Whether you are an omnivore, vegetarian or vegan, a bowl of curry, soup or stew can provide an easily digestible, low-maintenance and convenient meal that you can make in batches and freeze to pull out later."

SERVES	TIME	PLANTS
4	30 mins	13

METHOD

1. In a saucepan, fry the onions in oil for a few minutes until softened.
2. Add the spices, salt and tamarind paste and fry for a few minutes more. Then add the coconut milk, water and tomatoes and simmer gently for 5 minutes. Do not boil vigorously or the fats in the coconut milk will separate.
3. Add the sugar snap peas or mange tout and bring back to the boil.
4. Add the fish or tofu cubes to the pan and cook for a further 5 minutes until the fish or tofu is cooked through.

TO COOK WITH A SLOW COOKER

Place all the ingredients except the fish or tofu into a slow cooker, pour in enough water to cover them all and then cook on a high heat for four hours. The fish and tofu taste better here if cooked separately at the end and then added, but can be included in if you're leaving during the day whilst at work, to come home to. If you have more time, the spices can be fried separately first and then added in for more flavour.

Serving suggestion: serve the curry over courgetti, whole brown rice or quinoa.

⇄ SWAPS

Vegan: swipe the white fish with tofu

INGREDIENTS

- 2 onions, finely sliced
- 1 tbsp coconut oil
- 1 cinnamon stick
- 1 tbsp mustard seeds
- 2.5-5cm piece ginger, peeled and grated
- 2 chillis, deseeded and chopped
- 2-3 garlic cloves, minced
- 1 tsp cumin
- 1 tsp ground coriander
- 1 tsp garam masala
- ½ tsp ground turmeric or 2.5cm piece turmeric root, peeled and grated
- ½ tsp salt
- 2 tsp tamarind paste
- 400ml coconut milk
- 200ml water
- 2 tomatoes, diced
- 200g sugar snap peas or mange tout
- 250g white fish, skin removed, or 1 x 200g block firm tofu, pressed; cut into cubes

RECIPE BY CHARLOTTE WATTS

Charlotte is a nutritional therapist who qualified from the Institute for Optimum Nutrition (ION) in 2000 and went on to be a tutor and Year 3 programme leader there. Since, she has authored many books including: *Good Mood Food; The De-Stress Effect;* and *Yoga Therapy for Digestive Health*. She won the CAM (now IHCAN) Award for Practitioner of the Year in 2012.

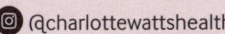 www.charlottewattshealth.com @charlottewattshealth

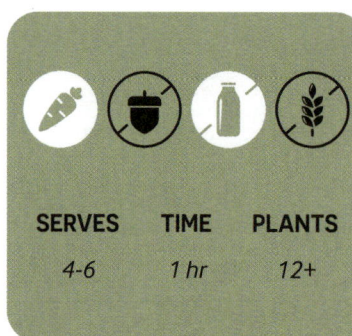

SERVES	TIME	PLANTS
4-6	1 hr	12+

INGREDIENTS

- 250g dried brown lentils
- 1 large sweet potato, peeled and diced
- 1 tbsp oil
- 2 onions, finely chopped
- 2 garlic cloves, crushed
- 1 tbsp curry powder
- 1 tsp turmeric
- 1 tsp ground coriander
- 1 tsp ground cumin
- 2 large carrots, grated
- Pinch of salt and milled pepper
- Juice and finely grated zest of half a lemon
- 2 tbsp fruit chutney, e.g. apricot or peach
- 1 tbsp Worcestershire sauce
- 50g raisins
- 2 eggs
- 250ml milk
- 5 bay leaves (optional)
- Fresh coriander, chopped, to garnish (optional)

LENTIL BOBOTIE

Mandy says: *"I recommend this recipe to my clients as it's fashioned on a popular South Africa mincemeat dish and even the most avid meat eater comes back for more!"*

METHOD

1. Place the lentils in a large lidded pot with enough water to cover them and simmer until soft (about 20 minutes), then drain.
2. Meanwhile, place the sweet potato in a large pot with enough water to cover it and simmer until soft (about 20 minutes), then drain.
3. Mash the sweet potato while hot and set it aside.
4. Lightly oil an ovenproof dish and preheat the oven to 180°C/160°C fan/gas mark 4.
5. In a pan, sauté the onion and garlic in a dash of oil for about 5 minutes until golden and caramelised.
6. Add the spices and cook for 1 minute, and then add the lentils and carrots and cook for a further 5 minutes.
7. Season with salt and pepper. Add the lemon juice, lemon zest, chutney and Worcestershire sauce. Mix in the mashed sweet potato and raisins.
8. Spoon everything into an ovenproof dish.
9. Whisk the eggs and milk together and season. Pour over the other ingredients and stud the dish with bay leaves, if using.
10. Bake for 30 minutes until golden and set in the middle.
11. Remove the bay leaves and garnish with coriander, if using.

Serving suggestion: serve with a side salad or vegetables.

 **SWAPS**

Vegetarian: choose a vegan Worcestershire sauce — many non-vegan bottles contain anchovies
Dairy-free: use a dairy-free milk

RECIPE BY MANDY VAN PROOIJEN

Mandy supports men and women with chronic disease to eat well, live well and transform their health. She is based in the coastal town of Pennington, South Africa, and specialises in the needs of older adults who want to live full, vibrant lives.

 www.feedyourhealth.co.za

LENTIL SHEPHERD'S PIE

Lucy says: *"Lentil shepherd's pie is an all-time family favourite that can easily be made vegan and gluten-free. You can adapt it to suit all dietary requirements and the base freezes really well. It's full of both polyphenol power and flavour."*

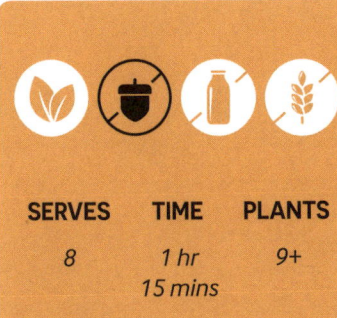

SERVES	TIME	PLANTS
8	1 hr 15 mins	9+

METHOD

1. If using dried lentils, put them in a pan, cover with water, add the sprig of sage, and simmer for 20-30 minutes until soft. Drain, rinse and put aside.
2. Boil the potatoes or sweet potatoes in water for 20-25 minutes until soft.
3. Preheat the oven to 190°C/170°C fan/gas mark 5.
4. In a pan, heat the olive oil and soften the onion for 10 minutes, making sure that it does not burn or brown.
5. Add the mushrooms, garlic and chilli flakes (if using) and cook for a couple of minutes until fragrant.
6. Add the tomato purée, chopped tomatoes, tamari or soy sauce, redcurrant jelly, red wine (if using), dissolved bouillon (if using), and lentils.
7. Mix well and simmer gently for 20 minutes until the sauce has reduced a little.
8. Season with salt and pepper and transfer to a large ovenproof dish. Sprinkle half of the parsley over the mixture.
9. Mash the potatoes well with the butter and milk, season with salt and pepper, and lay this over the top of the lentil mixture. Use a fork to create texture in the potato layer.
10. Bake in the oven for 30 minutes until golden brown on the top and bubbling around the edge.
11. Sprinkle with the remainder of the parsley.

Serving suggestion: serve with seasonal green vegetables.

INGREDIENTS

- 2 x 400g tins cooked green lentils (drained) or 300g dried green lentils
- Sprig of sage (for dried lentils)
- 6 medium potatoes or 3 sweet potatoes, peeled and chopped
- 2 tbsp olive oil
- 1 large onion, chopped
- 120g shiitake mushrooms, washed and chopped
- 2 garlic cloves, crushed
- Up to 1 tsp chilli flakes (optional)
- 1 tbsp tomato purée
- 2 x 400g tin chopped tomatoes
- 1 tbsp tamari or soy sauce
- 1 tbsp redcurrant jelly
- 100ml red wine (optional)
- 1 tsp vegetable bouillon mixed in a little water (optional)
- Salt and black pepper to taste
- Handful of parsley, chopped
- Knob of butter
- 1 tbsp milk of choice

 SWAPS

Vegan and dairy-free: use vegan alternatives to butter and milk
Gluten-free: use tamari instead of soy sauce

RECIPE BY LUCY BURNEY

Lucy is a nutritional therapist, author, food writer, keen kitchen gardener and mother of four children. She is the author of four cookery books on children's health: *Optimum Nutrition for Babies and Young Children; Immunity Foods for Healthy Kids; Superfoods for Healthy Kids;* and *Boost Your Child's Immune System.*

 www.lucyburney.co.uk   @lucyburneynutrition

MOROCCAN BEAN CASSEROLE

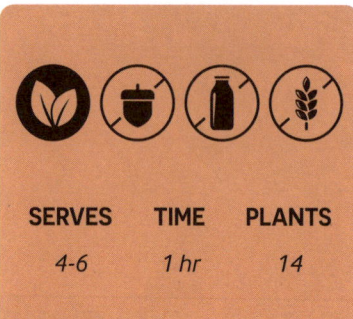

SERVES
4-6

TIME
1 hr

PLANTS
14

Samantha says: *"This recipe is easy to make, and you can leave it simmering on the hob. I recommend it to clients because it is straightforward to follow, can be batch cooked or slow cooked, freezes well, or can be eaten as leftovers the next day. The recipe is full of anti-inflammatory phytonutrients (turmeric, garlic, ginger) together with soluble and insoluble fibre from the beans and veggies which makes it a filling and tasty meal. The beans or chickpeas are beneficial for women as they are high in phytoestrogens."*

INGREDIENTS

- 1 tbsp olive oil or coconut oil
- 1 large red onion, evenly diced
- 2 garlic cloves, crushed
- 2.5cm piece fresh ginger, grated
- 1 tsp turmeric
- 1 tsp cumin
- 1 tsp sweet paprika
- 1 tsp ground cinnamon
- 1 tbsp tomato purée
- 3 medium carrots, peeled and evenly sliced
- ½ large butternut squash or 1 large sweet potato, peeled and evenly cubed
- 1 x 400g tin chopped tomatoes
- 400ml water
- 65g dates, chopped
- 65g unsulphured brown dried apricots, chopped
- 1 x 400g tin chickpeas, mixed beans or butterbeans, drained
- Salt and pepper to taste
- Handful of fresh parsley, chopped

METHOD

1. Heat the oil in large saucepan or lidded casserole dish and sweat the onion until soft but not brown.
2. Add the garlic, ginger, turmeric, cumin, paprika and cinnamon, and mix together.
3. Stir in the tomato purée, carrots, and squash or sweet potato, and mix well.
4. Add the tomatoes and water and bring to the boil. Then turn down the heat and simmer for 20 minutes.
5. Add the dates, apricots and tinned beans of your choice and simmer for a further 20-25 minutes until the fruit is soft and the sauce has thickened. Add salt and pepper to taste.
6. Sprinkle with parsley before serving.

Serving suggestion: serve with rice, buckwheat, pasta, couscous, quinoa or flatbreads.

⇆ **SWAPS**

Works well with any beans
The squash or sweet potato can be swapped for baby new potatoes
You can use other root veg such as parsnips or swede in lieu of carrots
The dried fruit can be swapped for prunes, raisins or sultanas

RECIPE BY SAMANTHA LEWIS

Samantha has been a registered nutrition practitioner since 2008 and is a lecturer and supervisor at the Institute for Optimum Nutrition (ION). Areas of special interest include digestive disorders, food intolerances and female hormone imbalances. Prior to training in nutrition, Samantha spent almost 20 years working in pharmaceutical clinical research as a project manager.

> Buckwheat is a grass, not a grain (no relation to wheat, and it's gluten-free). It is known for supporting blood sugar balance and is a rich source of the bioflavonoid rutin.

BUCKWHEAT RISOTTO

Charlotte says: *"Dark green leafy vegetables and salads like spinach, watercress and radicchio provide bitter flavours that get digestive juices flowing, including bile from the liver, that is needed to break down the fats that we eat."*

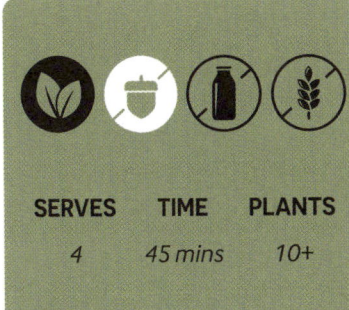

SERVES	TIME	PLANTS
4	45 mins	10+

METHOD

1. Fill a saucepan with 1 litre water and add the salt. Bring to the boil, add the peas and simmer for 1 minute.
2. Add the mint leaves and parsley leaves and blanche for a further 30 seconds.
3. Place 50g spinach in a sieve and pour the water from the pea pan over it, reserving the liquid in another pan.
4. Squeeze the liquid out of the peas, herbs and spinach, then blitz into a smooth purée in a food processor or with a stick blender. Set aside.
5. In the reserved pea cooking liquid, add any green veg offcuts, spring onion tops, herb stems and stock cube (if using), and gently simmer for 10 minutes to make a light vegetable stock.
6. In a new pan, dry toast the buckwheat kernels for 3 minutes, then remove.
7. Add oil to the empty pan and fry the shallots and garlic to soften for a couple of minutes before adding the buckwheat back to the pan.
8. Strain the stock, adding a little liquid to the buckwheat, shallots and garlic, and putting the rest back in its pan, with the seasonal green vegetables.
9. Blanche the green vegetables for slightly under its recommended cooking time. Then add the remaining liquid to the buckwheat pan and cook for 15-20 minutes, until the liquid has reduced and buckwheat cooked through.
10. Stir the pea purée through the risotto with the black pepper, and lemon zest and juice. Add the blanched greens to the risotto to warm back through.
11. Optionally whizz cashews and nutritional yeast into a coarse powder and sprinkle on top.

INGREDIENTS

- 1 litre water
- 1 tsp salt
- 110g frozen or fresh peas
- 10g mint leaves
- 15g parsley leaves
- 50g fresh spinach
- 200g seasonal greens plus off-cuts, chopped into florets or large bitesize pieces, if needed
- 1 bunch of spring onion tops
- 1 gluten-free stock cube (optional)
- 225g buckwheat
- 1-2 tsp oil
- 4 shallots, finely chopped
- 1 garlic clove, minced
- 1 tsp ground black pepper
- 1 lemon, zest of whole and juice of half

Optional vegan parmesan topping

- 15g cashews
- 2 tsp nutritional yeast flakes

⇆ SWAPS

Nut-free: omit the vegan parmesan topping, or swap it with real parmesan
Extra protein: serve with roast chicken
Vary the greens according to preference and seasonal availability

RECIPE BY CHARLOTTE WATTS

Charlotte is a nutritional therapist who qualified from the Institute for Optimum Nutrition (ION) in 2000 and went on to be a tutor and Year 3 programme leader there. Since, she has authored many books including: *Good Mood Food*, *The De-Stress Effect*, and *Yoga Therapy for Digestive Health*. She won the CAM (now IHCAN) Award for Practitioner of the Year in 2012.

 www.charlottewattshealth.com 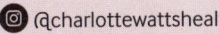 @charlottewattshealth

SERVES   **TIME**   **PLANTS**

1-2   35 mins   7

INGREDIENTS

- 40g uncooked quinoa
- 250ml water
- ½ gluten-free vegetable stock cube
- 1 tbsp rapeseed oil
- 50g courgette, diced
- ½ a small onion, finely chopped
- 1 garlic clove, crushed
- 6 cherry tomatoes, quartered
- 2 red peppers, whole
- 1 tbsp chopped parsley
- 30g soft goat's cheese, sliced

QUINOA AND COURGETTE STUFFED PEPPERS

Jackie says: *"This recipe is an immune powerhouse that's quick and easy to put together! The red pepper and parsley are rich in vitamin C. Together with the onions, garlic and tomatoes, there are a host of other antioxidants and anti-inflammatory compounds, such as lycopene and quercetin to keep you on great form. It's full of flavour and the quinoa packs a powerful protein punch to keep you going for longer."*

METHOD

1. Preheat the oven to 200°C/180°C fan/gas mark 6.
2. Rinse the quinoa in a sieve under cold running water and then add to a saucepan. Cover with 250ml water, add ½ stock cube, and bring to the boil. Reduce the heat and simmer for about 20 minutes or until the grains have opened up and are soft.
3. While the quinoa is cooking, heat the oil in a frying pan and add the courgette, onion, garlic and tomatoes. Cook gently for 10 minutes or until the vegetables have softened and then set aside on a plate.
4. When the quinoa is ready, strain it through a sieve and set aside.
5. Slice the top off the peppers and carefully trim the white flesh inside, removing the core and the seeds, so that you have a clean, smooth interior.
6. Cook the peppers in the microwave on a high setting for 3 minutes (or pop in the preheated oven for 20 minutes) so that they are soft and wilting but the structure hasn't collapsed.
7. In a bowl, mix together the cooked vegetables, quinoa and parsley and spoon it carefully into the peppers and top each pepper with sliced goat's cheese.
8. Put the peppers on a baking tray and put in the oven for 15 minutes.

⇆ **SWAPS**

Vegan and dairy-free: swap the goat's cheese for vegan soft cheese

---

RECIPE BY JACKIE LYNCH

Jackie is an award-winning nutritionist and founder of the WellWellWell clinic. She is the host of *The Happy Menopause* podcast and author of *The Happy Menopause: Smart Nutrition to Help You Flourish*; *Va Va Voom: the 10-Day Energy Diet*; and *The Right Bite: Smart Food Choices for Eating on the Go*.

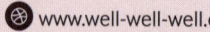 www.well-well-well.co.uk   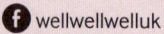 wellwellwelluk   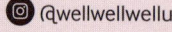 @wellwellwelluk

"

Quinoa is a brilliant source of plant protein and packed with fibre too, which is a winning combination to balance blood sugar and provide sustained energy. It's also naturally gluten-free, which makes it easy on the gut for anyone with a sensitive digestive tract.

"

QUINOA FALAFEL WITH AVOCADO AND TOMATO RELISH

Nicki says: *"These quinoa falafels are a tasty snack or lunch option and are easy to take on the go. Quinoa is a great way to up your protein intake, and it's also rich in nutrients and fibre, all great for your hormones and gut health."*

MAKES	TIME	PLANTS
12 falafels	*25 mins*	*11*

METHOD

1. Place all the falafel ingredients, except the quinoa, egg and oil, into a food processor and pulse until combined, leaving some texture.
2. Transfer to a bowl, add the quinoa and egg, and mix to make a sticky falafel dough. Form the falafel mixture into balls or press into patties.
3. Heat the oil in a pan and fry the falafels in batches until browned and crisp, for about 6-7 minutes per side depending on size.
4. Meanwhile, combine all the relish ingredients in a bowl and set aside. Serve with the falafels when cooked.

Serving suggestion: serve with pitta breads if you like (gluten-free if needed).

INGREDIENTS

For the falafel

- 1 x 400g tin chickpeas, drained
- 1 garlic clove
- ½ tsp cumin
- ½ tsp ground coriander
- 4 spring onions, thinly sliced
- 2 tbsp parsley, finely chopped
- Zest of 1 lemon
- 1 tbsp tahini
- Salt and pepper to taste
- 100g cooked quinoa
- 1 egg
- 1 tbsp extra virgin olive oil or coconut oil, for frying

For the relish

- 100g tomatoes, chopped
- 1 ripe avocado, diced
- 2 tsp parsley, chopped
- 2 spring onions, white and light green parts only, thinly sliced
- Juice of 1 lemon
- 1 tbsp extra virgin olive oil

⇄ SWAPS

Vegan: replace the egg with a flaxseed 'egg': 1 tbsp ground flaxseed mixed with 2½ tbsp water and let to rest for 5 minutes to thicken

RECIPE BY NICKI WILLIAMS

Nicki is an award-winning nutritionist, author and speaker, and a leading expert in women's health and hormones. She is the founder of Happy Hormones for Life, helping women of all ages to rebalance their hormones, reclaim their health and feel better than ever.

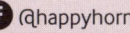 www.happyhormonesforlife.com **f** @happyhormonesforlife

GINGER SESAME TOFU STIR FRY

SERVES	TIME	PLANTS
2	2 hr 50 mins	13

INGREDIENTS

For the tofu

- 200g firm tofu
- 3 tbsp rice flour or gram flour
- 2 tsp ground ginger
- ½ tsp ground white pepper
- ½ tsp salt
- ¼ tsp ground chilli
- 1 tbsp coconut oil

For the sauce

- 7.5cm piece fresh ginger, peeled and finely chopped
- 2 garlic cloves, finely chopped
- 2 tsp honey or maple syrup
- 1 tbsp tamari
- 1 tbsp sesame oil
- Juice of 1 lime
- ½ tsp ground white pepper
- ½ tsp cracked black pepper

For the stir fry

- 2-3 tbsp sesame seeds
- 1 tbsp sesame oil
- ½ red onion, thinly sliced
- ½ red pepper, chopped into thin batons
- 3-4 sprigs purple sprouting broccoli or ¼ whole broccoli, chopped into bitesize pieces
- 1 carrot, peeled and julienned
- 5-6 spring onions, thinly sliced; the tops as rounds (to garnish), and whites as batons
- 1-2 handfuls spinach
- 10g fresh coriander, chopped

Charlotte says: *"This is the kind of dish that I find most soothing as an early evening meal when I need a bit of immune and detoxification support. Note I don't say 'immune boost' there as I am looking for regulation, and often that is to bring down immune responses that have been stuck in overactive mode (like inflammation or autoimmunity)."*

METHOD

1. Press the tofu for up to 2 hours – or buy extra firm and squeeze.
2. In a bowl, make the sauce: mix the ginger and garlic with the other sauce ingredients, leaving a little lime juice for garnish, and leave to infuse.
3. In a frying pan or wok, dry-toast the sesame seeds and then set aside.
4. Once the tofu has had sufficient pressing time to remove excess moisture, chop it into 1cm-thick batons.
5. In a bowl, mix the flour with the tofu seasoning and add the tofu batons. Mix well to ensure the tofu is thoroughly coated.
6. Heat the coconut oil in a frying pan or wok, and then add the coated tofu, frying for 1 minute on each side (4 minutes in total), until all the edges are golden and crisp. Set these aside on some absorbent kitchen paper to remove excess oil.
7. Clean the pan to remove any remaining flour, and then add the sesame oil. On a medium-high heat, stir-fry the red onion and pepper for a couple of minutes.
8. Add the broccoli with a couple of tablespoons of water, cook for a few minutes, and then add the carrot and cook for another 5 minutes.
9. Add the sauce to the pan and once this begins to bubble, add the spring onion batons (keep the tops for garnish), tofu and spinach, and cook for 1-2 minutes until the spinach wilts slightly.
10. Garnish with a generous sprinkle of toasted sesame seeds, spring onion tops, chopped coriander and the remaining lime juice.

Serving suggestion: serve hot on its own or with some wholegrain brown rice or buckwheat noodles if desired.

RECIPE BY CHARLOTTE WATTS

Charlotte is a nutritional therapist who qualified from the Institute for Optimum Nutrition (ION) in 2000 and went on to be a tutor and Year 3 programme leader there. Since, she has authored many books including: *Good Mood Food; The De-Stress Effect;* and *Yoga Therapy for Digestive Health.* She won the CAM (now IHCAN) Award for Practitioner of the Year in 2012.

 www.charlottewattshealth.com 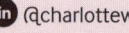 @charlottewattshealth

"

Cauliflower is an excellent choice for promoting cardiovascular health, reducing inflammation, and supporting the body's natural detoxification processes. It's full of fibre, antioxidants, glucosinolates and isothiocyanates, which together help protect the heart, combat oxidative stress, and activate liver enzymes.

"

CAULIFLOWER, CHICKPEA AND PEANUT CURRY

Nicola says: *"This is a very tasty way to incorporate chickpeas and cauliflower into your diet. Both are helpful for health but some clients are unsure what to do with them to make them enjoyable to eat! This recipe is also vegan, yet would hopefully appeal to anyone, including vegetarians and omnivores. It can be enjoyed as the main element of a meal but is also versatile enough to be a side dish. Using the pre-prepared sauce also makes this recipe accessible for someone who is time limited."*

SERVES	TIME	PLANTS
4	30 mins	8+

METHOD

1. Heat the coconut oil on a moderate heat in a large pan on the stove until melted, then add the onions and gently fry for 5 minutes, until soft and translucent.
2. Add the garlic, peanut butter, curry paste and tomato purée, and stir everything together. Gently cook for a couple of minutes, until you can smell the curry paste.
3. Add the cauliflower florets, chickpeas and coconut milk, and stir to combine. Cover with a lid and simmer for 15-20 minutes, or until the cauliflower has softened.
4. Taste the curry and add a pinch of salt and pepper to season, if desired. Garnish with the herbs, if using.

Serving suggestion: serve with wholegrain, black or wild rice, quinoa or more vegetables.

INGREDIENTS

- 1 tbsp coconut oil
- 1 medium onion, diced
- 2 garlic cloves, chopped
- 2 tbsp crunchy peanut butter
- 2-3 tbsp medium curry paste
- 1 tbsp tomato purée
- 1 medium cauliflower head, chopped into florets
- 1 x 400g tin chickpeas, drained and rinsed
- 1 x 400ml tin coconut milk
- Salt and pepper to taste (optional)
- 1 tbsp chopped fresh parsley or coriander, to garnish (optional)

⇆ SWAPS

The chickpeas can be swapped out for any other bean, such as butter beams or haricot beans. It also works well with added chicken for those who are not vegetarian or vegan

RECIPE BY NICOLA MOORE

Nicola is a renowned nutritionist and cognitive reframing specialist. She focuses on liberating clients and the wider public from negative behaviour and restrictive diets, promoting happier and healthier relationships with food, health and their bodies. Nicola is also dedicated to helping nutrition practitioners by running clinical support groups and accredited courses.

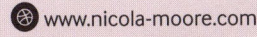 www.nicola-moore.com   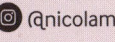 @nicolamoorenutrition

Sides

Garlic chilli sautéed kale

Garlicky cabbage

Green beans with almonds

GREEN BEANS WITH ALMONDS

SERVES	TIME	PLANTS
4	15 mins	2

1. Steam the green beans until cooked – about 8 minutes.
2. In a pan, heat the butter gently. Once melted, add the flaked almonds and stir until warmed through and slightly coloured.
3. Add the green beans into the pan. Stir until warm and coated in the butter, then tip into a serving dish and scrape out all the remaining butter and flaked almonds over the top.

GARLICKY CABBAGE

SERVES	TIME	PLANTS
2-6	15 mins	6

1. Take a thin slice off the base of the cabbage to give it a clean edge. Remove only the outer damaged or very dirty leaves. Slice the cabbage lengthways so that you have two halves, each of which retains the pointed shape.
2. Heat the oil in a pan. Place the cabbage cut-side down, to sear the leaves.
3. Turn down the heat as low as possible, drop the bay leaf, rosemary, thyme, garlic and butter into the oil beneath the cabbages, then put on a tight-fitting lid so that the cabbage gently cooks in the steam released from its own leaves. This should take about 10 minutes.
4. Remove the cabbage. Add the balsamic vinegar to the pan and heat through gently, stirring, then tip all of the juices over the cabbage (removing the bay leaf and any herb stalks), and serve with lemon juice over the top.

GARLIC CHILLI SAUTÉED KALE

SERVES	TIME	PLANTS
4	15 mins	4

1. Heat the oil in a large pan over a low heat. Add the onion and cook for 2-3 minutes, or until just beginning to soften.
2. Add the garlic and chilli and cook for 1-2 minutes, or until fragrant.
3. Add the kale and toss to coat using tongs. You may need to do this gradually, depending on the size of your pan. Cover with a lid and cook for 4-5 minutes, or until the kale is wilted.
4. Sprinkle with salt and pepper to serve.

INGREDIENTS

Green beans with almonds

- 300g any kind of green bean
- 15g flaked almonds
- 1 tbsp butter (or olive oil)

Garlicky cabbage

- 1 hispi/pointed cabbage
- 1 tbsp olive oil
- 1 dried bay leaf
- 1 small sprig of fresh rosemary
- 1 small sprig of fresh thyme
- 3-4 garlic cloves
- 2 tbsp butter (or olive oil)
- 1 tbsp balsamic vinegar
- ½ tbsp lemon juice

Garlic chilli sautéed kale

- 2 tbsp extra virgin olive oil
- ½ small onion, finely diced
- 3 garlic cloves, crushed
- Pinch of chilli flakes
- 500g curly kale, stalks removed, roughly chopped
- Salt and black pepper to taste

GREEN BEANS & GARLICKY CABBAGE RECIPES BY KATIE SHEEN

Katie has taught nutrition since 2009, initially on the MSc Nutritional Therapy course at the University of Worcester and now at CPD events. Her private practice focuses on mindfulness for health, pain and anxiety. She is the creator of *Appreciating Windowsills* and a contributing author for *Tears Become Rain*.

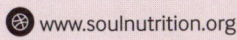 www.soulnutrition.org 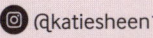 @katiesheen1

GARLIC CHILLI SAUTÉED KALE RECIPE BY CHARLOTTE GRAND

See page 39 for Charlotte's bio.

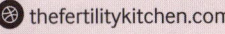 thefertilitykitchen.com
@thefertilitykitchen

PEANUT BUTTER SLAW

SERVES 10+

TIME 30 mins

PLANTS 12

Sally says: *"This recipe is one of my daughter's favourites. She has always been a little wary of new foods, but when she came back from a friend's house explaining how delicious their slaw was, I had to find out more. Armed with some of the key ingredients, I developed our own family version of this really delicious side dish. I enjoy adding some sliced chilli on top of mine; my husband and elder daughter add sriracha. We call it 'Laura slaw' in our house after my friend who introduced me to it. It is great served with chicken drumsticks, thighs or wings."*

INGREDIENTS

For the salad

- 90g curly kale, finely chopped
- 330g red cabbage, shredded
- 230g carrots, grated
- 1 red pepper, finely sliced
- ½ red onion, finely diced

For the dressing

- 3 tbsp peanut butter
- 3 tbsp rice vinegar
- 1 tbsp lime juice
- 1 tbsp soy sauce
- 1 tbsp oil of your choice
- 1 tbsp honey
- 1 garlic clove, grated
- 2.5cm piece fresh ginger, grated
- Pinch of chilli flakes or small red chilli, chopped

For the garnish

- 80g almonds, flaked or sliced
- Large handful of fresh coriander, chopped

METHOD

1. Combine the salad vegetables in a large bowl.
2. Combine the dressing ingredients in a jar or bowl, and shake or stir well to ensure they're all mixed together.
3. Pour the dressing over the salad vegetables and mix well.
4. Gently toast the almonds in a dry pan for a couple of minutes until golden brown.
5. Sprinkle the garnish ingredients on top of the dressed slaw and serve.

 **SWAPS**

Vegan: swap the honey with maple syrup
Gluten-free: swap the soy sauce with tamari

RECIPE BY SALLY TEMPLE

Sally is a registered nutritional therapist and wellbeing coach, and specialises in ME/CFS in her private practice. She is also a lecturer and module coordinator for Clinical Practice at the Institute for Optimum Nutrition (ION).

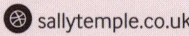 sallytemple.co.uk

Peanut butter slaw

Rainbow slaw

SERVES	TIME	PLANTS
6	15 mins	9+

RAINBOW SLAW

Suzy says: *"I love this recipe because it can be adapted for whatever vegetables you need to use up, it's quick and easy to prepare, and it's really colourful and full of beneficial phytonutrients.*

"Undressed, this slaw keeps for up to three days in the fridge. It works well in a packed lunch or as a side dish with fish or meat."

INGREDIENTS

- ¼ red or white cabbage, shredded or sliced
- 2 carrots, grated
- 1 beetroot (raw or cooked), grated, julienned or chopped
- 1 white onion, finely sliced
- 1cm piece fresh ginger, grated
- Handful of mixed fresh herbs, chopped (e.g. coriander, parsley, chives and dill)
- Handful of walnuts and pumpkin seeds, to serve (optional)
- Handful of beetroot and carrot greens, chopped, to serve (optional)

For the dressing

- 1 tsp Dijon mustard
- 3 tbsp apple cider vinegar
- 9 tbsp extra virgin olive oil
- Pinch of salt and pepper
- Heaped tsp pesto
- Heaped tbsp natural yoghurt
- ½ tsp honey

METHOD

1. Prepare the vegetables and herbs using a processor, grater or mandolin, or by chopping with a sharp knife, then put them all into a large bowl and mix.
2. Combine the dressing ingredients in a jar and shake well, or lightly whisk in a bowl.
3. Pour the dressing over the salad before serving. Scatter over the walnuts, pumpkin seeds and chopped beetroot and carrot greens, if using.

⇆ SWAPS

"You can add in other vegetables such as celeriac, fennel and sprouts, and fruits such as apples or pears. The beets can be cooked or raw – cooked gives a softer slaw. Swap the ginger for fennel seeds. Use any herbs you have available. This is a super versatile dish."

Vegan and dairy-free: use dairy-free pesto and yoghurt. For vegan, use maple syrup instead of honey
Nut free: leave out the walnuts

Don't like the dressing? Use a good quality mayonnaise to dress

---

RAINBOW SLAW & SAUERKRAUT RECIPES BY SUZY WYLD

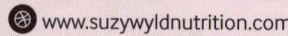 www.suzywyldnutrition.com @suzywyld_nutrition

SAUERKRAUT

Suzy says: *"This is a great recipe for using up the veg you don't know what to do with. When there are only one or two people in a household, a cabbage can be too big. Creating a ferment means there's no food waste.*

"Fermented foods are particularly good for our gut microbiome, although take care if you have histamine intolerance. If you're not used to eating fermented foods, just try a teaspoon at a time.

"The most important thing with ferments is that you use 2% salt to add to the dry weight of vegetables. You can use any veg, any herbs and any spices. Start with just cabbage. Be adventurous!"

METHOD

1. Mix the chopped, sliced and julienned vegetables, keeping the whole cabbage leaf separate. Add the fennel seeds or ginger.
2. Weigh and add 2% salt, e.g. for exactly 400g vegetables, use 8g salt.
3. Mix the salt into the vegetables with your hands until they become wet.
4. Pack into a sterile Kilner jar, pressing down hard. The vegetables should produce their own water to make the brine. Use the whole cabbage leaf to press into the top of the jar to keep the vegetables under the brine.
5. Put the jar on the side in the kitchen, in a dish. The vegetables will start to ferment and create bubbles which need to be allowed to escape, so burp your ferment every day for about 5 days. Then place it in the fridge. The longer you keep the fermented vegetables, the stronger the taste. Sauerkraut can last months in the fridge, as long as the vegetables remain submerged. If mould appears, discard.

MAKES	TIME	PLANTS
1 large jar	5 days	3+

INGREDIENTS

- 400g mixed raw vegetables, chopped, sliced or julienned, e.g. cabbage, carrots, beetroot, onion
- 1 whole cabbage leaf
- 1 tsp fennel seeds or 2cm piece fresh ginger, grated
- Approx. 8g sea salt

Suzy lives and works in rural Hertfordshire with her husband and cat, with occasional visits from her wonderful children. Suzy sees clients both online and face to face in her clinic, which is in the Hertfordshire/Essex/Cambridgeshire borders. She is passionate about food and enjoys preparing meals for friends and family, trying new recipes and eating out. Suzy works with her clients to discover the root cause of their symptoms, guiding and supporting them to bring about positive long-term changes to their health.

> Carrots are a great source of carotenoids which our bodies convert to vitamin A, and other antioxidants including lutein and zeaxanthin, which are well known to support eye health. They contain plenty of soluble fibre for gut health and to help us keep fuller for longer.

Sauerkraut

Carrot pickle

CARROT PICKLE

Jo says: "*I was inspired to create this pickle recipe after attending a fermentation workshop by George Upshall, head chef at Wild Flor Brighton.*

"*Carrot pickle is easy to make and can enhance many a meal. It has a delicious tangy and spicy flavour and works well with salads, sandwiches, cheese boards, tacos, curries and more. Fermented foods have many health benefits including containing more bioavailable nutrients and providing beneficial microbes to support gut and immune health. Garlic and carrots both have prebiotic qualities, meaning they help feed our friendly gut bacteria. All the spices, ginger and turmeric are highly beneficial as they provide a variety of anti-inflammatory antioxidants and phytonutrients.*"

MAKES — 1 jar
TIME — 7-10 days
PLANTS — 10

METHOD

1. Preheat the oven to 180°C/160°C fan/gas mark 4.
2. Sterilise an ovenproof jar and lid by washing it well and placing it in the oven for 15 minutes. Let it cool.
3. Heat the oil in a frying pan and gently toast the dry spices for 1-2 minutes.
4. In a bowl, mix the toasted spices, grated carrot, ginger, garlic and chilli.
5. Weigh the mixture and add 2% of the mixture weight of salt, e.g. if the mixture weighs 300g, use 6g salt. Mix the salt in well.
6. Press the mixture into the sterilised jar.
7. Seal with the lid and leave somewhere warm and dark for 7-10 days. It's best to place it on a plate if the jar is very full, as some juice may leak out.
8. Open the lid every 3 or 4 days to allow air to escape. You should see some bubbles forming; this is normal as it ferments. Then store it in the fridge.

INGREDIENTS

- 2 tsp olive oil
- 2 curry leaves
- 1 tsp curry powder
- ½ tsp turmeric powder
- ½ tsp cumin seeds
- 1 tsp coriander seeds
- ½ tsp ground black pepper
- 1 cardamom pod
- 300g carrots, grated
- 2 tsp fresh ginger, grated
- ½ garlic clove, grated
- 1 chilli, sliced
- Approx. 6g salt (see method 5)

 **SWAPS**

Play around with the chilli and other spices to suit your palate

RECIPE BY JO MAJITHIA

Jo has been in clinical practice for over 20 years, with extensive experience supporting clients with their digestive and hormonal health. She has worked in nutrition education at the Institute for Optimum Nutrition (ION) and for corporate wellbeing programmes. She now provides practitioner support in functional testing as Head of Clinical Education at Regenerus Labs. Jo lives on the south coast and loves swimming in the sea.

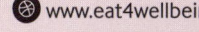 www.eat4wellbeing.co.uk @eat4wellbeing

SERVES	TIME	PLANTS
4	45-50 mins	9+

ROAST AUBERGINE AND CAULIFLOWER WITH TAHINI YOGHURT

May says: *"This is a great low-carb vegetarian dish that can be served as a main with a fresh green salad or as a side with other dishes. It's full of a variety of plants, fibre, protein and healthy fats from the yoghurt, nuts and tahini. The roasted vegetables bring a depth of flavour while the herbs keep it fresh. I love this salad served with slow-roast lamb and a fennel and lentil green salad with a lemon olive oil dressing."*

INGREDIENTS

- 2 small/1 large aubergine, cut into 1cm-thick rings
- 1 cauliflower, cut into florets
- 4 tbsp olive oil
- 2 tsp Baharat spice mix or sumac
- 1 tsp sea salt

For the tahini yoghurt sauce

- 100g tahini
- 80ml water
- 1 garlic clove, minced
- Juice of 1 lemon
- 250g live Greek yoghurt
- 1 tsp dried mint
- Pinch of sea salt

To top

- 15g flaked almonds, toasted
- Small handful of fresh dill, parsley and/or mint, chopped
- 1 tsp Turkish red pepper flakes
- 1 tsp Baharat spice mix or sumac
- Drizzle of olive oil
- Pinch of sea salt

METHOD

1. Preheat the oven to 200°C/180°C fan/gas mark 6.
2. Put the aubergine and cauliflower into a bowl and add the olive oil, spices and sea salt. Mix well to ensure the vegetables are evenly coated.
3. Arrange the vegetables on a baking tray and cook for around 30 minutes, turning halfway through.
4. Meanwhile, combine the tahini, water, garlic, lemon juice, yoghurt, dried mint and salt to make the sauce. Mix well.
5. To toast the nuts, put them in a dry frying pan over a medium heat for 3-5 minutes until golden, stirring occasionally.
6. To serve, spread the tahini yoghurt sauce on a serving dish and top with the aubergines and cauliflower. Top with the flaked almonds, herbs and spices, a drizzle of olive oil, and a pinch of sea salt.

⇆ SWAPS

Vegan and dairy-free: swap the yoghurt for a vegan alternative, such as coconut or almond
Nut-free: leave out the almonds or replace them with pumpkin seeds

RECIPE BY MAY KNIGHT

May is a registered nutritional therapist and type 1 diabetic. She works closely with clients to address a variety of health concerns, with a special interest in blood sugar regulation and digestive health. Her approach to working 1:1 involves delving into the root cause of health issues, rather than simply focusing on symptoms.

 www.mayknightnutrition.com 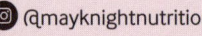 @mayknightnutrition

> "
>
> Cauliflower and other cruciferous vegetables are a rich source of the antioxidant plant compound sulphurophane, which has been shown to have powerful health benefits including supporting liver function and detoxification.
>
> "

> I have many herbs in my herb garden. Some are medicinal, like comfrey, and some are more for culinary use, like chives and parsley. Parsley is a fantastic herb as it regenerates. Every time you cut it, it regrows. It is quite prolific and will regrow all summer. Parsley is also high in vitamins A, K and C, and full of powerful antioxidants.

LEBANESE TABBOULEH

Carla says: *"This recipe is from my childhood. My grandmother used to make it for me when I would visit her. It was a real labour of love as she used to dice everything by hand. These days I cheat and use a food processor – she would be horrified! I also once substituted bulgur wheat with quinoa when I made it for her. This was met with great disapproval, but it improved the nutritional value of the recipe."*

SERVES	TIME	PLANTS
4-6	35 mins	7

METHOD

1. Put the bulgur wheat into a bowl and cover with about 3 inches of boiling water. Leave for 20 minutes. It will double in size after absorbing the water.
2. Put the parsley and mint into a mixing bowl, and then add the red onion, spring onion and tomato, trying to keep as much water/juice out of the tomato as possible.
3. Drain any water out of the bulgur wheat, add to the salad and mix well.
4. Dress with olive oil, lemon juice and salt, adjusting quantities according to taste.

INGREDIENTS

- 40g bulgur wheat
- 2-3 bunches curly parsley, stems removed and finely chopped
- 15 fresh mint leaves, finely chopped
- ½ red onion, finely chopped
- 1 spring onion, finely chopped
- 1 large beef tomato, finely chopped
- 5 tbsp extra virgin olive oil
- Juice of 1 large lemon
- Salt to taste

⇆ SWAPS

Gluten-free: swap bulgur wheat with quinoa
No fresh mint? Use dried mint instead
Use more or less onion according to taste

RECIPE BY CARLA BATES

Carla is a nutritional therapist who qualified in 2023. She runs her business, Weighting for a Change, from her home in Weymouth, providing online nutritional therapy sessions and specialising in sustainable weight loss. Her approach is not about restricting food, but adding variety and colour to a plate to ensure a range of nutrients. She also educates people about macronutrients (fat, carbohydrates and protein) to nurture them on their weight-loss journey. She addresses limiting beliefs around food and focuses on behaviour change, as someone who understands the struggle personally.

🌐 www.weightingforachange.co.uk

SERVES | **TIME** | **PLANTS**
4-8 | 40 mins | 12

INGREDIENTS

- 1 vermicelli rice noodle nest
- 12 round rice paper wraps
- 1 avocado, thinly sliced
- 1 carrot, shredded or grated
- ½ cucumber, finely julienned
- 6 spring onions, thinly sliced lengthways
- ¼ red cabbage, shredded
- 1 soft round lettuce head, washed and leaves separated
- Handful of peanuts, chopped
- Handful each of mint and coriander leaves, chopped
- Drizzle of sesame oil

For the satay dipping sauce

- 2 tbsp crunchy peanut butter
- 2 tsp hoisin sauce
- 1-4 tbsp boiling water

For the Nuoc Nam dipping sauce

- 2 limes, juiced
- 40g caster sugar
- 40ml fish sauce
- 1 small garlic clove, crushed
- 1 red chilli, finely minced

SUMMER ROLLS

Anna says: *"I have used this recipe for the best summer's day lunch, after school snack, potluck plate, bake sale offering, drinks canapé and fun DIY dinner where everyone can make their own. They're an inclusive dish (gluten- and dairy-free) and I've yet to find anyone who dislikes them — it's all about the dipping sauces!"*

METHOD

1. Pour a kettle of boiling water over the noodles in a large bowl and leave to stand for 3 minutes. Drain, rinse in cold water, toss in a drizzle of sesame oil and set aside.
2. Fill another large bowl with boiling water and set this aside to cool slightly.
3. Mix together the satay sauce ingredients, using water from the kettle a little at a time until you get the right dipping consistency, and set aside.
4. Nuoc Nam dipping sauce: add the lime juice and sugar to a jar and microwave without a lid for 15-20 seconds to dissolve the sugar (or give it a really long stir). Then add the fish sauce, garlic and chilli, put the lid on, and shake to combine.
5. Place the remaining ingredients around a chopping board, with the bowl of hot water to your side. Take a wrap and fully immerse it in the hot water. Remove it swiftly and place it on a chopping board. Slice one side-edge off the circle with a knife, about 2.5cm in from the edge, so you have one straight side.
6. Take a pinch of each filling ingredient (avocado, carrot, cucumber, spring onion, cabbage, lettuce, peanuts, noodles and herbs) and put it near the bottom of the circle.
7. Place one lettuce leaf next to your fillings so the top spills over the side of the straight edge.
8. Now starting at the bottom, lift up the damp edge of the wrap and fold it over the filling ingredients. Next, move to the curved side without the lettuce leaf, and lift that up and over the side of the filling. Now roll the covered filling 'sausage' up towards the top edge.
9. Repeat with the rest of the wraps.

Serving suggestion: stand or lie the wraps on a plate or shallow bowl with the floppy lettuce poking out the top, with your two dipping sauces.

 **SWAPS**

Vegan: swap fish sauce for vegan 'fish' sauce
Nut-free: swap peanuts for seeds or omit them entirely; skip the satay sauce
Gluten-free: use a gluten-free hoisin sauce or tamari

RECIPE BY ANNA ADSETTS

Anna wants to take the hairshirt out of healthy. She runs Food Confidence, supporting people in reaching good health through a positive relationship with food. Anna uses her chef skills and training from the Institute for Optimum Nutrition (ION) to promote an exciting, individualised approach to eating.

 www.foodconfidence.co.uk   @food.confidence

> Add some leftover chicken, cooked prawns or grilled tempeh slices to up the protein and turn these into a complete meal.

GOJI BERRY AND SMOKED PAPRIKA HUMMUS

Karine says: *"Elevate your special occasions with this delightful twist on classic hummus. Combining the rich creaminess of traditional hummus with a tangy hint of surprise, this appetiser is as nourishing as it is delicious. Packed with protein, fibre, vitamins and minerals, it's a delectable way to savour the best of both taste and nutrition."*

SERVES **TIME** **PLANTS**

6 20 mins 6+

METHOD

1. Soak the goji berries for around 15 minutes in water.
2. Combine the remaining ingredients in a food processor and blitz until smooth.
3. Drain the goji berries, then add them to the food processor and process until almost smooth.
4. Transfer to a bowl and garnish with extra goji berries and walnuts, if desired.

Serving suggestion: serve with crudités and/or toasted pitta bread (gluten-free if needed).

INGREDIENTS

- 50g dried goji berries (plus extra to serve, optional)
- 1 x 400g tin chickpeas, drained and rinsed
- 1 x 400g tin cannellini beans, drained and rinsed
- 1 tbsp tahini
- 2 tbsp olive oil
- 50g walnuts (plus extra to serve, optional)
- 3 tbsp lemon juice
- 1 tbsp smoked paprika
- 2 pinches of salt

⇆ **SWAPS**

Nut-free: omit the walnuts

RECIPE BY KARINE STEPHAN

Karine is a registered nutritional therapy practitioner specialising in women's health, with a particular interest in hormone health, as well as ADHD. Her passion is to support women to make positive, sustainable changes through diet and lifestyle. Karine loves experimenting with food and helped her husband start Palace Culture, an award-winning plant-based cheese alternative company.

 www.happylivingnutrition.co.uk   @happylivingnutrition

ROAST GARLIC AND BEAN DIP

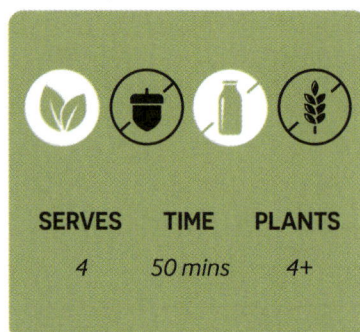

SERVES 4

TIME 50 mins

PLANTS 4+

INGREDIENTS

- 1 large head of garlic
- 4 tsp olive oil
- 1 x 400g tin cannellini beans, drained
- 75g low-fat soft cheese
- 1 tbsp lemon juice
- 1 tbsp olive oil
- Salt and freshly ground black pepper to taste
- 4 sundried tomatoes in oil, finely chopped (optional)
- Selection of raw vegetables, e.g. celery hearts, peppers, baby corn, mange tout, radish and carrots, to serve

Lorna says: *"This is a change from hummus as a snack or dip and I suggest it as an alternative to encourage eating more pulses. It is beneficial because it's high in fibre, and garlic is purported to have many healthful properties: protecting the heart, an antioxidant, lowering blood pressure and cholesterol, anti-cancer and antibacterial, anti-coagulant and anti-mucus. Roasting garlic and making a paste softens the flavour so you can use more in dishes than the average one or two cloves in recipes."*

METHOD

1. Preheat the oven to 200°C/180°C fan/gas mark 6.
2. Remove the papery outer skin from the head of garlic without separating the cloves. Cut off 1 cm from the stem end. Place on a piece of foil, drizzle over 1 tsp of olive oil and loosely wrap in the foil. Alternatively, use an earthenware garlic roaster. Bake for 40 minutes, until the cloves are soft. Leave to cool.
3. Tip the beans into a sieve, rinse under cold water and drain.
4. Once baked, squeeze the garlic to remove the cloves from the skins. Put into a blender with the soft cheese, beans, lemon juice and remaining oil. Purée until smooth, and then season with salt and pepper.
5. Add the sundried tomatoes to the dip, if using, and stir.
6. Prepare the vegetables of your choice, e.g. trim the leaf end from the celery hearts, then cut each one lengthways into six or four depending on their size; remove seeds from peppers and cut into wide strips; trim stalks from mange tout; peel and cut carrots into sticks.
7. Put the dip into a serving dish and serve with the vegetable crudités.

⇆ **SWAPS**

Vegan and dairy-free: substitute soft cheese for a dairy-free alternative

RECIPE BY LORNA RHODES

Lorna trained as a home economist and worked as a cookery writer and food stylist for 40 years creating recipes for books, food companies and PR campaigns. She always promoted healthy eating, but then chose to study nutritional therapy, and loves working with clients to improve their health with dietary changes.

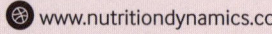 www.nutritiondynamics.co.uk 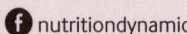 nutritiondynamics

SOCCA BREAD (FARINATA)

Milena says: *"Apart from the fact that it looks impressive on a plate or as a contribution to a dinner party, I recommend this to clients who are starting a gluten-free diet. It's a very easy and versatile recipe that can be used in many different ways and a great alternative to processed flatbreads from the supermarket. It can also be cooked in batches and stored in the freezer. Using chickpea flour makes a great alternative to wheat flour as it has a lower glycaemic index and is higher in protein, so helpful with blood sugar management. This recipe can be used as flatbreads or pizza bases. You can also cook this on the hob first and finish off under the grill. The cooking time may vary but it's easy to check when it's done as the batter should be fully set."*

SERVES	TIME	PLANTS
4	45 mins	1+

INGREDIENTS

- 135g chickpea flour
- 240ml water
- 2 tbsp olive oil, plus more for the pan
- ½ tsp fine sea salt, plus extra salt flakes for sprinkling
- Several pinches of herbs, such as oregano or rosemary (optional)
- 1 tbsp sundried tomatoes, thinly cut (optional)
- 2 tsp za'atar (optional)

METHOD

1. Mix the chickpea flour, water, olive oil and salt in a bowl. Use a hand blender or whisk to make sure all the mixture is smooth and clump-free.
2. Leave the mixture to rest for at least 15 minutes before cooking. You can even do this the night before to use in the morning.
3. Preheat the oven to 200°C/180°C fan/gas mark 6. About 5 minutes before ready to cook, turn the grill element on (if you have one) and place a large cast iron pan close to the grill to warm up. If you don't have a cast iron pan, use a baking tray instead.
4. Take the pan out of the oven when hot and pour on a tiny bit of olive oil to coat the surface.
5. Pour the chickpea flour mixture into the pan and swirl it around to form a large thick pancake covering the whole surface of the pan. Aim for 4-5 mm thick.
6. Place the pan under the grill and cook for 5-8 minutes until the top is slightly blistered and the mixture is all set. If you see that the top is burning, place the pan a bit lower down from the grill.
7. Use a wooden flat spatula to gently detach the socca bread from the pan and transfer to a large plate.
8. Sprinkle on salt flakes and optional seasonings, such as herbs, sundried tomato slices or zaatar.
9. Cut into triangles or squares, or serve as a gluten-free pizza base or wrap.

RECIPE BY MILENA MASTROIANNI

Milena is a proud graduate of the Institute for Optimum Nutrition (ION) and a member of ION's CPD team. She is also a registered nutritional therapist with a busy clinic working mostly with women's health, including fertility and pregnancy nutrition support. Milena loves showing clients that it can be easy and tasty to optimise our nutrition.

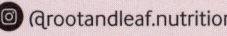 www.rootandleafnutrition.com @rootandleaf.nutrition

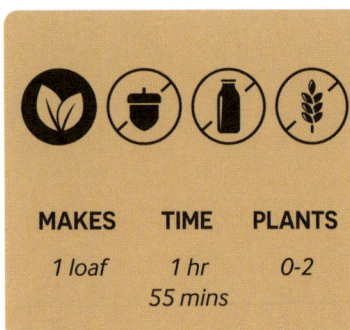

MAKES — 1 loaf

TIME — 1 hr 55 mins

PLANTS — 0-2

INGREDIENTS

- 300g Shipton Mill gluten-free white bread mix + 40g Freee plain white flour, OR 340g Freee plain white flour
- 100g quinoa flour (Shipton Mill)
- 100g buckwheat flour (Freee)
- 1 tbsp psyllium husk (optional; do not include in the presence of constipation or bloating)
- 1 tbsp ground golden flaxseed (optional)
- 2 tsp gluten-free baking powder
- 2 tsp pink salt

Wet ingredients

- 1 sachet Bioreal organic yeast (7g)
- 600ml warm water

THE GUT COACH GLUTEN-FREE LOAF

Claire says: *"I designed this easy to prep gluten-free bread loaf because it's quick and faff-free for single parents like me. It is gluten-free because I had an intestinal parasite a number of years ago and decided to remove gluten in support of immunity. It is particularly beneficial because it contains ground gold flax, a source of soluble fibre to boost the large intestine gut bacteria. It also contains quinoa flour for a protein source. It is a mix-only recipe – no kneading or nurturing – and has a sourdough like texture without being chalky or slimy – no gums!*

"Even if you don't eat a gluten-free diet, this bread is worth a try given how easy it is to make and its fibre and protein content. All you need to do is mix the recommended ingredients together, rise and bake. A sandwich made from this bread has the potential to keep you going throughout the afternoon and may reduce the desire to reach for sugary snacks.

"The recommended brands of flour and yeast I use in my recipe are tried and tested and may be easier to digest for people with gut symptoms."

METHOD

1. Mix the dry ingredients together.
2. Dissolve the yeast in 600ml warm water and stir until fully dispersed.
3. Pour the yeast water into the dry ingredients and stir well for a few minutes.
4. Use a bread scraper or spatula to fully incorporate all flour and liquid together. It should be the consistency of a very thick batter.
5. Cover with a tea towel and leave in a warm place to rise for 1-2 hours.
6. Turn out into a greaseproof paper-lined loaf tin.
7. Cover with a tea towel, and let it rise again for 20 minutes.
8. Preheat the oven to 210°C/190°C fan/gas mark 6.
9. Bake for 50 minutes or until the bottom sounds hollow upon tapping with a wooden spoon. Then turn out onto a wire tray and leave until fully cooled.

RECIPE BY CLAIRE BOUTSIAVARAS

Claire, the Gut Coach Nutritionist, is a nutritional therapist with professional backgrounds in education, health coaching and holistic massage therapies. She reaches a wide range of clients with gut health support, to rebalance from digestive problems that may also affect their mood and skin and cause pain in muscles and joints. Claire is also a trauma-informed coach.

 www.thegutcoachnutritionist.com thegutcoachnutritionist @thegutcoachnutritionist thegutcoachnutritionist

Desserts

> We all like a sweet treat every now and again, which is why I created this sweet, gooey version of a classic, with the added goodness of nutritious nuts, dark chocolate and dates. I often bring this to potluck parties, and people can't believe it has no refined sugar in it!

VEGAN MILLIONAIRE'S SHORTBREAD

Catherine says: *"This is such a favourite with my clients, friends and family! It takes a little while to make, but it feels like such a treat... and unlike traditional desserts, it's rich in protein and healthy fat so is less likely to send your blood sugar on a rollercoaster.*

"You can use any nuts for the base, or nut butter for the caramel (e.g. almond or hazelnut butter). If you're gluten free, make sure you use gluten-free oats."

SERVES	TIME	PLANTS
14	45 mins	6+

METHOD

To make the bottom layer

1. Blitz the nuts, oats, dates and salt in a food processor. Any processor with an s-blade works well. If you don't have a processor, use ground nuts or chop everything as finely as you can.
2. Melt the tahini with the coconut oil. Pour into the dry ingredients and give them another blitz. You can leave it chunky if you prefer or make it smoother.
3. Push the mixture into a square or rectangular baking tray, with a loose bottom or lined with baking paper. Put in the freezer.

To make the caramel

4. Melt the coconut oil with the molasses (or maple syrup) and water. Add the dates and salt and allow the mixture to heat until it starts to bubble.
5. Take the bubbling mixture off the heat and stir in the smooth nut butter. Then blitz it all in a food processor or using a small hand blender. Pour this over the frozen base and put it all into the fridge. The caramel goes fairly firm, but not hard.

To make the top layer

6. Melt the chocolate in a bowl over a pan of boiling water. Add a pinch of salt if you wish. After the first two layers have had about 15 minutes in the fridge, spread over your chocolate and put back in the fridge to set.
7. Once set, turn out your millionaire's shortbread and slice into squares.

Best kept in the fridge.

INGREDIENTS

For the bottom layer

- 100g pecans or cashews
- 100g almonds
- 50g oats (gluten-free if needed)
- 4 dates, stones removed
- Pinch of salt
- 1 tbsp tahini (or any nut butter)
- 2 tbsp coconut oil

For the caramel layer

- 100g coconut oil
- 1 tbsp blackstrap molasses (or maple syrup)
- 50ml water – about 3 tbsp
- 150g dates (about 12 dates), stones removed and snipped into small pieces
- Pinch of salt
- 150g peanut/almond butter

For the top layer

- 100g dairy-free dark chocolate
- Pinch of salt (optional)

RECIPE BY CATHERINE JEANS

Catherine is a functional nutritional therapist, supporting children and adults of all ages with digestive health, hormone balance, weight management, stress relief and neurodiversity. Her ethos is to empower clients towards a lifetime of good health, using simple, everyday food and lifestyle changes.

 www.thefamilynutritionexpert.com   familynutritionexpert   @catherine_jeans

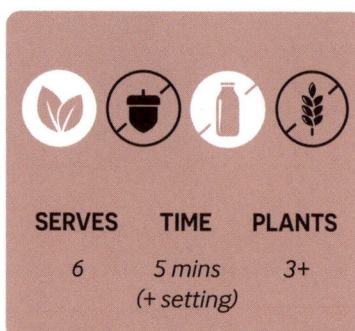

SERVES 6

TIME 5 mins (+ setting)

PLANTS 3+

INGREDIENTS

- 1 x 400ml tin full-fat coconut milk
- 3 tbsp cocoa or cacao powder
- 1 tsp vanilla extract or paste
- 140g soft dates, pitted

To top (optional)

- Dark chocolate, grated
- Desiccated coconut
- Fresh raspberries

COCO-CHOC MOUSSE

Katharine says: *"This is a super simple and quick dairy-free sweet treat, which is light, silky and delicious. It's sweetened naturally with dates, which are a great source of soluble and insoluble fibre, aiding digestion and promoting bowel regularity. Alongside this natural sugar, coconut milk adds to the depth of flavour and is packed full of medium-chain triglycerides, which can support weight management by reducing appetite and boosting metabolism."*

METHOD

1. Put all of the ingredients into a blender or food processor and pulse until smooth.
2. Divide between 6 ramekins and keep in the fridge for a couple of hours to set.
3. To serve, top with grated chocolate, desiccated coconut and fresh raspberries.

⇆ **SWAPS**

Vegan and dairy-free: opt for dairy-free, vegan-friendly chocolate

---

RECIPE BY KATHARINE TATE

Katharine is an award-winning registered nutritional therapist and the founder and director of The Food Teacher. She combines her unique education and nutrition expertise to offer schools, organisations and individuals advice, education programmes, practical workshops and clinical consultations. She has written and published several books: *Heat-Free & Healthy*, the award-winning *No Kitchen Cookery for Primary Schools*, and a series of mini-books; and has also co-authored the award-winning *Now We're Cooking! Delivering the National Curriculum Through Food*. She has also launched a programme of Young Chef awards for schools, which support delivery of the curriculum and nutrition education.

 www.thefoodteacher.co.uk   thefoodteacheruk   @thefoodteacher

GLUTEN-FREE BANANA CAKE

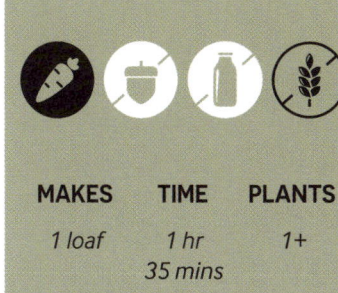

Emine says: *"This is a delicious gluten-free cake for everyone. It is very easy to prepare, and can be made with or without nuts, though walnuts are a great source of omega-3 fatty acids. Bananas are rich in potassium and give the cake a silky smooth texture."*

MAKES **TIME** **PLANTS**

1 loaf *1 hr* *1+*
         35 mins

METHOD

1. Preheat the oven to 190°C/170°C fan/gas mark 5 and line a loaf tin with baking paper.
2. Mix the coconut oil or butter with the coconut palm sugar using an electric mixer until the mixture changes colour and becomes thicker.
3. Add the eggs one at a time. Mix for another 4-5 minutes until the mixture becomes fluffy.
4. Add about a third of the flour into the mixture and continue beating until combined.
5. Add the bananas, vanilla extract, bicarbonate of soda and salt, and mix.
6. Finally add the remaining flour and mix. The mixture should be a thick liquid consistency. If it is thicker than this, add water. If it is too liquid, add an extra spoon of flour.
7. Add walnuts, if using, and stir well.
8. Pour the mixture into the loaf tin and bake in the oven for approximately 1 hour and 15 minutes. From 40 minutes, insert a cocktail stick from time to time, and take the cake out of the oven when the stick comes out completely clean.

INGREDIENTS

- 200g coconut oil or butter
- 100g coconut palm sugar
- 2 free-range eggs
- 350g chestnut flour
- 4 bananas, mashed
- 1 tsp vanilla extract
- 2 tsp bicarbonate of soda
- ½ tsp Himalayan salt
- 150g walnuts, roughly chopped (optional)

⇆ SWAPS

Nut-free: replace chestnut flour with gluten-free plain flour and leave out the walnuts
Dairy-free: Use coconut oil, not butter
Money-saving: replace coconut palm sugar with dark brown sugar

RECIPE BY EMINE BASAK

Emine is a nutritional therapist who graduated from the Institute for Optimum Nutrition (ION) in 2015. In 2018, she also completed the Institute of Function Medicine (IFM)'s AFMCP qualification. Emine is a member of IFM, the British Association for Nutrition and Lifestyle Medicine (BANT) and the Complementary and Natural Healthcare Council (CNHC). Emine's main interest is disease prevention through nutrition and strengthening the immune system. She works with clients with differing needs and offers solutions to reduce their symptoms through targeted and personalised nutritional therapy and lifestyle changes.

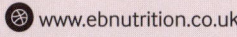 www.ebnutrition.co.uk

APPLE AND RHUBARB CRUMBLE

SERVES	TIME	PLANTS
4-6	30 mins	8+

Nicky says: *"Green apples are full of pectin, which is the stuff that makes jam congeal. From a nutrition perspective, it is thought to be excellent for digestive health as it may repair and maintain the digestive tract lining. Pectin is released when apples are cooked, making this apple and rhubarb crumble great for your digestion."*

INGREDIENTS

- 4 green eating apples, unpeeled, sliced or chopped
- 1 bunch (approx. 7-8 sticks) of rhubarb, chopped into thumb-sized pieces
- 1 tbsp allspice
- 120g rolled oats
- 125g chilled butter, cubed, plus extra for buttering the dish
- 8 dates, roughly chopped
- 25-50g of 70-85% dark chocolate, roughly chopped
- 20g walnuts
- 20g shredded coconut
- 1 tsp sugar (optional)

METHOD

1. Preheat the oven to 190°C/170°C fan/gas mark 5.
2. Smear butter around the base of a pie dish using kitchen towel.
3. Put the apple and rhubarb pieces into an ovenproof dish and sprinkle over the allspice and a dash of water. Mix well.
4. Place the dish in the oven for around 20-30 minutes to soften the fruit.
5. Whilst the fruit is in the oven, make the crumble topping: put the oats, butter, dates, dark chocolate and walnuts into a food processor and blend/pulse for short bursts until the mixture resembles very chunky sand grains.
6. Once the fruit is soft, remove from the oven and pour the crumble over the top. Use a spoon to spread the crumble evenly over the fruit.
7. Sprinkle the shredded coconut over the top, along with the sugar if using for extra sweetness.
8. Return the dish back to the oven, increase the temperature to 200°C/180°C/gas mark 6, and cook for 20-25 minutes until the topping is lightly browned.

Serving suggestion: serve with Greek yoghurt or cream.

⇄ SWAPS

Vegan and dairy-free: swap the butter for coconut oil and use dairy-free chocolate. Serve on its own or with coconut yoghurt
Nut-free: omit the walnuts
Gluten-free: use gluten-free oats
No rhubarb: just use double the apples

RECIPE BY NICKY CLARK

Nicky is a qualified nutritional therapist working in Sydney City, Australia. Nicky sees clients for private consultations, runs online programmes and delivers talks, workshops and presentations. Nicky has a practical and no-nonsense approach when it comes to nutrition that many describe as 'refreshing'.

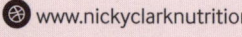 www.nickyclarknutrition.com 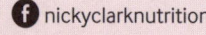 nickyclarknutrition 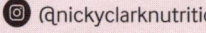 @nickyclarknutrition

> " Did you know there is a type of rhubarb called 'forced rhubarb' which is grown in the dark and picked by candlelight? Forced rhubarb is sweeter than normal as the plant puts all of its energy (and therefore sweetness) into growing the stalk taller to search for light! "

EASY NO-BAKE FUDGE BALLS

Karine says: *"These simple, no-bake fudges are an indulgent alternative to ultra-processed treats. Made with nutritious ingredients and bursting with rich flavours, they combine the natural sweetness of medjool dates with the earthy nuttiness of walnuts. They are the perfect balance of taste and nutrition, which makes them an ideal choice for satisfying your sweet tooth."*

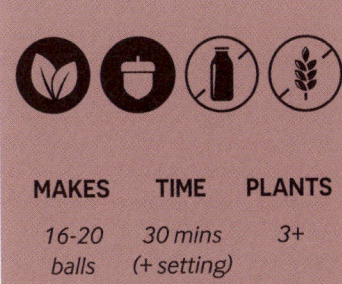

MAKES	TIME	PLANTS
16-20 balls	30 mins (+ setting)	3+

METHOD

1. Grind the walnuts in a food processor then slowly add the dates, cocoa/cacao powder and salt until it forms a dough. (You can add a splash of water if needed to help it stick together.)
2. Divide the mixture into about 16-20 portions and roll into small balls in the palms of your hand.
3. If using, roll the balls in your coating of choice (e.g. raspberry or strawberry pieces or desiccated coconut).
4. Put the balls into a container and leave to set in the fridge for a couple of hours.

INGREDIENTS

- 110g walnuts
- 11 medjool dates, pitted
- 40g cocoa or cacao powder
- Pinch of sea salt
- 2 tbsp freeze dried raspberry or strawberry pieces, or desiccated coconut, to coat (optional)

RECIPE BY KARINE STEPHAN

Karine is a registered nutritional therapy practitioner specialising in women's health, with a particular interest in hormone health, as well as ADHD. Her passion is to support women to make positive, sustainable changes through diet and lifestyle. Karine loves experimenting with food and helped her husband start Palace Culture, an award-winning plant-based cheese alternative company.

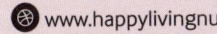 www.happylivingnutrition.co.uk @happylivingnutrition

SERVES	TIME	PLANTS
4-6	2 hr 45 mins	6

BLACK RICE AND COCONUT PUDDING

Diana says: *"I like to recommend this to my clients as a dessert or breakfast, because it is easy to cook in advance and can really set you up for the day. It can be eaten hot or cold too. Black rice is a real nutrient and antioxidant powerhouse, it is high in plant protein and rich in fibre, iron and polyphenols, which are simliar to those found in red grapes and blueberries. One of the magic antioxidants is called anthocyanin, known for its anti-inflammatory properties. I chose vitamin C-rich seasonal fruit because they make a refreshing combination with coconut milk and support the absorption of plant-based iron."*

INGREDIENTS

- 200g black rice, soaked in water for at least 2 hrs, even better overnight
- 400ml full-fat coconut milk
- 200ml water
- ½ vanilla pod, scraped out seeds and pod
- 40g dried apple slices, finely chopped
- Pinch of salt
- 3 tbsp coconut chips/flakes, toasted
- 1 pear, sliced
- 1 tbsp pomegranate seeds

METHOD

1. Drain the rice, rinse well and place in a medium-sized pot. Keeping 2 tbsp of coconut milk for garnish, add the rest along with the water, vanilla seeds and pod, chopped apple and pinch of salt.
2. Bring to a boil, reduce the heat and simmer, covered, for 30-40 minutes, stirring occasionally until the rice is cooked and the liquid is mostly absorbed. Add some water if needed. You want to have a creamy consistency in the end. Cooking times vary, so check the package instructions (note: soaked rice may take less time to cook).
3. In the meantime, toast the coconut chips: warm them in a frying pan at medium heat without oil until slightly golden brown and crisp.
4. Once the rice is cooked, leave it to sit covered for another 5 minutes before serving. Garnish with fruit, coconut milk and toasted coconut chips.

⇄ SWAPS

No dried apples: use dates or apricots
No coconut chips: use plain or toasted nuts
Experiment with fruit: kiwi, berries, apples, passion fruit, mango, papaya...
More sweetness: use 60g chopped dried dates instead of 40g dried apple slices, use sweeter fruit on top, and sweeten with honey or maple syrup

RECIPE BY DIANA WARRINGS

After graduating from the Institute for Optimum Nutrition (ION) in 2016, Diana went down the culinary nutrition route. She took further training at Leiths School of Food and Wine, and Hofmann Culinary School in Barcelona, and has been working as a holistic chef, recipe developer and content producer ever since. Diana recently returned to practice and now runs a private online clinic in Berlin, where she is also offering cooking workshops.

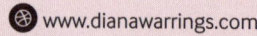 www.dianawarrings.com 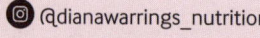 @dianawarrings_nutrition

> Plant-based iron is not as bioavailable as iron derived from animal products. However, vitamin C can support iron absorption, so it helps to combine your dishes with vitamin C-rich foods, such as fresh fruit or vegetables.

“

Alpha-linolenic acid (ALA) is a plant-based omega-3 fatty acid found in foods like flaxseeds, chia seeds, and walnuts. It is essential for heart health and must be converted in the body to EPA and DHA, the more active forms of omega-3s found in fish oil. Include a tablespoon of ground flaxseeds or chia seeds in your daily diet to boost your intake.

”

RAW OMEGA CHOCOLATE BROWNIES

Mike says: *"This recipe is a delicious and nutritious alternative to a biscuit or sugary brownie. It makes a great afternoon snack or a treat for the lunchbox and it's rich in vitamins, minerals and plant-based omega-3 fatty acids to support brain health."*

MAKES	TIME	PLANTS
16 brownies	15 mins (+ setting)	6

METHOD

1. Place all the ingredients in a food processor and blitz until the consistency of a fine crumb (a minute or two).
2. Dump out the crumb onto a large sheet of greaseproof paper and use the paper to kneed the crumb, folding and squeezing it in on itself until the sugars from the dates and the oils from the nuts and seeds begin to come together into a dough.
3. Between two sheets of greaseproof paper rollout the dough to about 2.5cm thick and shape into a square, roughly 15cm x 15cm.
4. Place in the fridge for a couple of hours and then cut into small pieces.

INGREDIENTS

- 200g pitted medjool dates
- 100g toasted coconut flakes
- 50g walnuts
- 50g pumpkin seeds
- 2 tbsp cacao powder
- 1 tbsp maple syrup
- 1 tsp cinnamon
- 1 tsp coconut oil
- Pinch of sea salt

⇆ SWAPS

Nuts and seeds: you can swap the walnuts, pumpkin seeds and coconut for any of your favourite nuts and seeds, e.g. brazil nuts, cashews and sunflower seeds; or pecans, almonds and sesame seeds. For a nut-free option, just use seeds

Fruit: you can also replace some of the dates with other dried fruit, e.g. figs, apricots or prunes

RECIPE BY MIKE MURPHY

Mike is an experienced and passionate health educator. His areas of clinical interest include cardiovascular health, reversing type 2 diabetes and longevity. In addition to his clinical practice, Mike is the chief nutritionist for Nutrable, the UK's only dedicated nutrition support platform for advancing employee wellness.

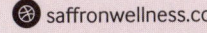 saffronwellness.com 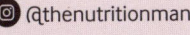 @thenutritionman

MAKES	TIME	PLANTS
20-24 cookies	30 mins	4

INGREDIENTS

- 200g ground almonds
- 5 pitted medjool dates (approx. 100g)
- 2 level tsp white miso paste
- 1 large egg
- 1 tsp vanilla extract
- 100g buckwheat flour
- 50g coconut oil or butter, melted
- ½ tsp baking powder
- 75g dark chocolate (70-85%)

MISO AND ALMOND COOKIES

Lucy says: *"Miso cookies are a family favourite and a fabulous blend of sweet and salty whilst only relying on natural ingredients. They're popular with children and adults alike – a messy triumph to make with all the family!"*

METHOD

1. Heat the oven to 180°C/160°C fan/gas mark 4.
2. Add all the ingredients except chocolate to a food processor and blitz to form a dough.
3. Form small balls in the palm of your hand and place on a baking sheet.
4. Flatten with a fork to form a criss-cross pattern.
5. Bake for 10-12 minutes until turning golden brown. Do not allow to burn.
6. Place on a rack to cool.
7. Meanwhile, break the chocolate into pieces in a heatproof bowl. Pour some boiling water into a pot that's slightly smaller than the bowl and place the bowl on top; it shouldn't be touching the water. Bring the water to a simmer, stirring the chocolate constantly until it melts.
8. Drizzle the cookies with the melted chocolate.
9. Allow to set and place in a cookie jar.

 **SWAPS**

Vegan: use coconut oil instead of butter, use vegan chocolate, and swap the egg with a flax or chia egg (1 tbsp seeds and 3 tbsp water, mixed and left to sit for 15 minutes before using)
Dairy-free: use coconut oil instead of butter, and dairy-free chocolate
Gluten-free: use gluten-free baking powder and check miso is gluten-free

RECIPE BY LUCY BURNEY

Lucy is a nutritional therapist, author, food writer, keen kitchen gardener and mother of four children. She is the author of four cookery books on children's health: *Optimum Nutrition for Babies and Young Children; Immunity Foods for Healthy Kids; Superfoods for Healthy Kids;* and *Boost Your Child's Immune System.*

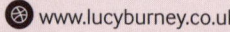 www.lucyburney.co.uk 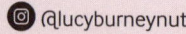 @lucyburneynutrition

" These bars are packed with slow-release carbohydrates (oats) or complete protein (quinoa), both of which are ideal for supporting musculoskeletal health and energy levels without giving too much of a blood sugar spike. And the darker the chocolate or cacao powder you use, the greater the flavanol antioxidant content, which may help reduce post-exercise inflammation in the body, "

BANANA OAT BARS

Kate says: *"I have put this recipe in the second of my series of my Vegetables Galore children's books because the ingredient combinations and options offer a treat worthy of the sweet-toothed, alongside a variety of plant-based foods, antioxidants, natural sweetening agents, slow releasing carbohydrates and proteins."*

MAKES	TIME	PLANTS
6-10 bars	40 mins	5+

METHOD

1. Preheat the oven to 200°C/180°C fan/gas mark 6.
2. Place all the ingredients except for the optional items into a mixing bowl and mash and mix them together until they form an almost solid 'goo'.
3. Add the optional ingredients, if using, and give the whole mixture one last combining stir.
4. Line a baking tray with baking parchment/paper, then carefully spoon the mixture onto the tray. Spread it out to about 1½ cm thick.
5. Bake in the oven for approximately 25 minutes, checking it after 20 minutes (especially if using quinoa flakes). If it still looks uncooked, leave for another 5 minutes – it should be golden in colour and neither solid nor too squidgy in the middle. After 25 minutes, repeat your checks every 3 minutes. When cooked, remove from the oven and allow to cool until cold enough to eat.
6. Slice the mixture into as many square or rectangle portions as you wish.

This snack can be stored in an airtight container for up to five days.

⇄ SWAPS

Vegan and dairy-free: use nut butter instead of unsalted dairy butter and make sure the chocolate chips are dairy-free. For vegan, swap the honey for maple syrup
Nut-free: swap the nut butter for unsalted dairy butter
Gluten-free: use gluten-free oats or quinoa flakes. The texture of the bars will be a little different with quinoa flakes but the instructions remain the same

INGREDIENTS

- 2 bananas (ideally one with a yellower skin and one with greener skin), peeled and sliced
- 25g dried apricots, chopped into small pieces
- 35g dark chocolate chips or 1 tbsp dark cocoa/cacao powder (preferably 70%)
- 1 tbsp honey
- 100g porridge oats or quinoa flakes
- 50g nut butter of choice (or unsalted dairy butter)
- Palmful of dried goji berries (optional)
- 1 tsp cinnamon (optional)

RECIPE BY KATE TAYLOR

Kate graduated from the Institute for Optimum Nutrition (ION) in 2022, and has since gone on to add ReCODE 2.0 Dementia & Alzheimer's specialist training to her nutritional therapy repertoire. She now specialises in providing nutritional therapy for clients with brain or cognitive health priorities, alongside nutrition for skin health (of which Kate has personal experience).

 www.eatdrinkthinknutrition.co.uk   @eat.drink.think.nutrition   kate-eat-drink-think-nutrition-7527a19b

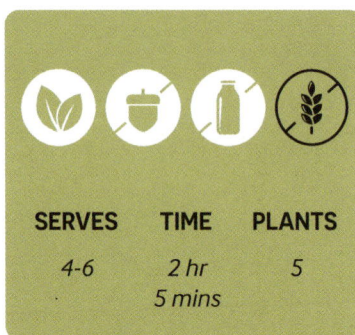

SERVES
4-6

TIME
2 hr
5 mins

PLANTS
5

INGREDIENTS

- 15g unsalted butter
- 100g pudding rice
- 25g caster sugar
- ½ tsp nutmeg, freshly grated
- 700ml full fat milk
- 25g soft dried dates, pitted and chopped
- 1 tbsp balsamic vinegar
- 250g ripe strawberries, hulled and chopped
- 1 tbsp chia seeds
- 1 tbsp pistachio nuts, chopped, to serve

RICE PUDDING WITH STRAWBERRY CHIA JAM

Joy says: *"I like to offer simple, good food; not too many ingredients and very easy to make. This is a delicious low-sugar jam made with chia seeds, which provide important omega-3 fats in the diet."*

METHOD

1. Preheat the oven to 160°C/140°C fan/gas mark 3. Butter a 1½ litre ovenproof dish.
2. Pour in the rice, sugar and nutmeg, followed by the milk and mix well.
3. Bake for 2 hours, or until the rice is just tender and the milk is brown on top.
4. Meanwhile, to make the jam, place the dates in a pan with the vinegar and 2 tbsp water and cook over a low heat, stirring to form a lumpy paste.
5. Add the strawberries and continue to cook on a low heat for 4-5 minutes. Then remove the pan from the heat, stir in the chia seeds and mash them into the soft strawberries with a fork or masher.
6. Spoon the mixture into a small jar, and once it has cooled, seal with a lid. The jam can be stored in the fridge for up to a week.
7. Serve the rice pudding topped with the jam and pistachio nuts.

 SWAPS

Vegan and dairy-free: use plant-based alternatives to butter and milk
Nut-free: omit the pistachio nuts

RECIPE BY JOY SKIPPER

Joy is a registered nutritionist and certified chocolate taster who is mad on sport (doing it rather than watching it), and passionate about sustainability. All of these things are used in her goal to help people to eat and taste the best food they can, supporting optimal health along the way. Joy is also a food photographer and stylist, and she has photographed all the recipes in this cookbook.

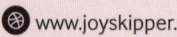 www.joyskipper.co.uk @thejoyfulskipper

Drinks

Spiced turmeric and cacao latte

Dandelion and almond mocha

DANDELION AND ALMOND MOCHA

SERVES	TIME	PLANTS
2	10 mins	3+

Belinda says: *"Dandelion root coffee is naturally caffeine-free and provides some delicious bitter flavours as well as a nutty sweetness due to the presence of the fibre inulin. This comforting and warming drink is a good source of polyphenols, minerals and protein, has probiotic benefits, and is nourishing and satisfying."*

1. Add all the ingredients into a saucepan and heat to simmering point.
2. Whizz with a stick blender to blend and create a creamy, frothy texture. Check for flavour and adjust if necessary.

Vegan: use maple syrup to sweeten, if desired

SPICED TURMERIC AND CACAO LATTE

SERVES	TIME	PLANTS
2	5-7 mins	3+

Mike says: *"Turmeric has over 4,000 years of medicinal use. Apart from it tasting delicious, the spices in this warming drink are anti-inflammatory and high in antioxidants, vitamins and minerals."*

1. Put all the ingredients into a small saucepan on a medium heat and gently whisk until just before simmering.
2. Pour into your favourite mugs and enjoy. Tip: You may need to mix the drink towards the end to avoid all the spices being left at the bottom.

No coconut: swap the coconut drink with your favourite alternative, e.g. almond, oat, rice, etc. You may also prefer 50:50 boiling water to milk

INGREDIENTS

Dandelion and almond mocha

- 500ml almond milk, unsweetened
- 1 heaped tbsp smooth almond nut butter
- 1 tbsp dandelion root coffee
- 2 tsp cocoa powder
- Pinch of cinnamon (optional)
- Dash of honey or maple syrup, if required

Spiced turmeric and cacao latte

- 500ml coconut drink
- 2 tsp turmeric powder
- 1 tsp cacao powder
- ½ tsp cinnamon
- Pinch of finely ground black pepper
- Pinch of sea salt
- 1 tsp coconut oil
- 1 tsp maple syrup (optional)
- 2 bruised cardamom pods (optional)

DANDELION AND ALMOND MOCHA RECIPE BY BELINDA BLAKE

Belinda is an experienced registered nutritional therapist, lecturer and clinical supervisor at the Institute for Optimum Nutrition (ION). She is a passionate foodie and, in addition to her clinic work, runs practical hands-on workshops for children and adults interested in learning new cooking skills, trying their hand at fermentation, or learning how to incorporate seasonal wild food into their meals.

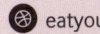 eatyourselffab.wordpress.com 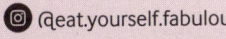 @eat.yourself.fabulous

SPICED TURMERIC AND CACAO LATTE BY MIKE MURPHY

Mike is an experienced and passionate health educator. His areas of clinical interest include cardiovascular health, reversing type 2 diabetes and longevity. In addition to his clinical practice, Mike is the chief nutritionist for Nutrable, the UK's only dedicated nutrition support platform for advancing employee wellness.

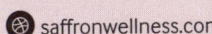 saffronwellness.com 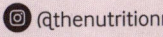 @thenutritionman

WATER KEFIR

Belinda says: *"If you haven't tried making your own probiotic drink, it is well worth giving it a go, especially if you have kids or teenagers in the house. Once you have the equipment and kefir grains, you can produce a ready supply of healthy fizzy drinks that feed the microbiome as much as the tastebuds."*

MAKES	TIME	PLANTS
1 litre	30-60 mins prep	3+

INGREDIENTS

- 1 sachet of water kefir grains* (approx. 1-2 tbsp)
- 2 tsp organic dried fruit (e.g. raisins and dates)
- ½ lemon
- 65g sugar (not honey, stevia or xylitol)
- 1 slice of fresh ginger
- 750ml-1 litre filtered chlorine-free water (I use boiled water that has been left overnight to cool)

Equipment

- 1 litre glass jar

*I purchase my grains from Happy Kombucha: happykombucha.co.uk

METHOD

Stage 1 Fermentation: 15 minutes prep/24-72 hours to ferment

1. In a large glass jar, stir the sugar into the filtered water until it has dissolved (the water should be cool or room temperature before adding the kefir grains, never hot), then add the kefir grains, dried fruit, lemon and ginger.
2. Cover the jar with a tea towel and secure with an elastic band. Leave to ferment for between 24 and 72 hours – usually 72 hours, but fermentation will be quicker in warmer weather. You will know that fermentation is occurring when you can see little bubbles floating to the surface and the dried fruits are bobbing up and down. At this point, taste the liquid. If it is still sweet, then it may need to be left for another day or so.
3. Once ready to use, strain the liquid using a sieve and remove all the pieces of fruit – you can either eat these (delicious!) or give your compost a treat. The kefir grains can then be used again for your next fermentation.

Stage 2 Fermentation: 15-60 minutes prep/24-48 hours to ferment

4. At this stage, you can experiment with flavour, adding 170ml-250ml juice per litre of kefir (see *Pineapple Kefir* recipe).
5. Pour the kefir into brewing bottles, ensuring you leave at least 2cm free at the top for gas expansion, and store in a cardboard box. (After years of doing this and hearing too many stories of exploding glass bottles, I now opt to use plastic bottles instead – not so great for the environment, but much better for my nerves!) Using bottles with a screw top will also allow you to release some of the gas gently and in a more controlled way.
6. Pop the lid on the bottles and leave at room temperature for 24-48 hours. Check your bottles regularly.
7. When you are happy with the flavour and fizziness, put the bottles in the fridge and enjoy! Refrigerating the kefir will slow down fermentation.

RECIPE BY BELINDA BLAKE

Belinda is an experienced registered nutritional therapist, lecturer and clinical supervisor at the Institute for Optimum Nutrtion (ION). In addition to her clinic work, Belinda runs practical workshops for children and adults interested in learning new cooking skills, trying their hand at fermentation or learning how to incorporate seasonal wild food into their meals.

 eatyourselffab.wordpress.com 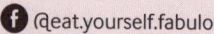 @eat.yourself.fabulous

Water kefir

Roasted pineapple kefir

Turmeric and ginger wellness shot

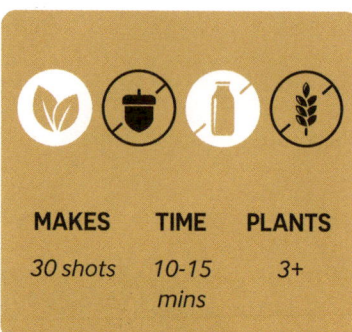

MAKES	TIME	PLANTS
30 shots	10-15 mins	3+

INGREDIENTS

- 100g fresh ginger, peeled and finely grated
- 50g fresh turmeric, peeled and finely grated (or 20g turmeric powder)
- 10g black pepper
- Juice of half a lemon
- 20g manuka honey (optional)
- Plain kefir drink (unsweetened), as needed (see Water Kefir recipe, page 180)

Add more spices to enhance flavour and boost health benefits, e.g. ceylon cinnamon, cardamom, nutmeg, cayenne pepper, fennel seeds

TURMERIC AND GINGER WELLNESS SHOT

Rakhi says: *"From my earliest memories, whenever I had a sniffle, my mother would whip up a soothing ginger and turmeric concoction to keep the bugs at bay. I've since added my own twist to this time-honoured remedy. This recipe is packed with anti-inflammatory benefits from the ginger and turmeric, while black pepper boosts the absorption of turmeric's curcumin. Lemon adds immune-supporting vitamin C and a burst of zest. With the addition of kefir, this versatile paste also supports gut health and digestion. The paste can enhance the flavour and nutritional profile of teas, soups, smoothies, stews or curries, adding a vibrant and healthful twist to your favourite recipes."*

METHOD

1. In a bowl, thoroughly mix the ginger, turmeric, black pepper and lemon juice. If using honey, add it now and mix until you achieve a smooth, consistent paste.
2. Transfer the paste into a clean, airtight glass jar and store in the fridge until needed.
3. Each morning, mix about 5ml (roughly 1 tsp) of the ginger-turmeric paste into a cup or shot glass of kefir. Adjust the quantity to taste for a personalised wellness shot.
4. Stir well to ensure the paste blends smoothly with the kefir, creating a rich, golden gut-loving shot.

Keep the paste in the fridge for 4-5 days or freeze in small ice cube trays (it may stain it yellow), and then use as needed in stews, smoothies, curries or soups, or add a cube each morning to a mug of hot water.

 SWAPS

Vegan and dairy-free: use plant-based or water kefir. For vegan, omit the honey or replace it with maple syrup

RECIPE BY RAKHI LAD

Rakhi's passion for nutrition stems from her personal health journey, grappling with challenges like PCOS, type 2 diabetes, lupus and hypothyroidism. Having successfully managed her own health setbacks, she came to appreciate the power of nourishing the body from within, regardless of genetic makeup. Now, she's dedicated to using her insights to help her clients achieve greater longevity and wellbeing through tailored nutritional therapy.

 www.healthologyhub.com   healthologyhub   @healthologyhub

ROASTED PINEAPPLE KEFIR

MAKES	TIME	PLANTS
1 litre	1 hr prep	5+

Belinda says: *"This is my daughter's favourite recipe and was her introduction to the world of fermented drinks. It is probiotic and packed full of flavour and phytonutrients, but if you don't want the faff of roasting and juicing a fresh pineapple, you can simply add 250ml of pressed pineapple juice to water kefir for its second fermentation."*

1. Preheat the oven to 200°C/180°C fan/gas mark 6.
2. Top and tail the pineapple, then trim off the skin.
3. Cut the flesh (including the core) into chunks about 2cm in size (it just needs to fit down the feeding tube of a juicer).
4. Place on a lined baking sheet and sprinkle with the sugar, grated ginger and crushed cardamom pods.
5. Roast in the oven for around 30 minutes until golden, turning the pineapple over halfway through cooking. If you don't want to roast it in the oven, you could also grill or griddle the pineapple (or cook in an air-fryer).
6. When cooked, allow the pineapple to cool before passing through a juicer.
7. Add the pineapple juice to the water kefir and bottle – following the steps for Stage 2 Fermentation in the *Water Kefir* recipe.

MULLED APPLE JUICE

SERVES	TIME	PLANTS
4	35 mins	8

Belinda says: *"The ingredients for this warm, spiced drink can be adapted to suit your tastes and what you can find in the cupboard (or can forage from the garden)."*

1. Combine all the ingredients in a saucepan. Bring to a boil, then cover and reduce the heat.
2. Simmer for 20 minutes and allow the flavours to infuse.
3. Strain through a sieve to remove the spices and enjoy warm.

INGREDIENTS

Roasted pineapple kefir

- 750ml water kefir (made to Stage 1 Fermentation – *see page 180*)
- 1 small pineapple
- 2 tbsp brown sugar
- 2cm piece ginger root, grated
- 6 cardamom pods, crushed

Mulled apple juice

- 1 litre pressed apple juice
- 1 lemon, one half zested and one half sliced
- 2 slices ginger root (or 1 tsp grated ginger for a fiery flavour)
- 4 cloves
- 1 cinnamon stick
- Sprig of rosemary
- Sprinkling of fennel seeds, lightly crushed
- 4 cardamom pods, lightly crushed

RECIPES BY BELINDA BLAKE

Belinda is an experienced registered nutritional therapist, lecturer and clinical supervisor at the Institute for Optimum Nutrition (ION). She is a passionate foodie and, in addition to her clinic work, runs practical hands-on workshops for children and adults interested in learning new cooking skills, trying their hand at fermentation or learning how to incorporate seasonal wild food into their meals.

 eatyourselffab.wordpress.com 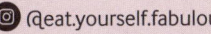 @eat.yourself.fabulous

Mulled apple juice

Elderflower and rhubarb spring spritzer

ELDERFLOWER AND RHUBARB SPRING SPRITZER

Belinda says: *"This recipe is based upon an oxymel – a blend of fruit-infused vinegar sweetened with honey. Using raw honey and vinegar without heating produces a delicious probiotic syrup which can be used in salad dressings or made into a cooling and refreshing drink."*

SERVES	TIME	PLANTS
1	15 mins prep	2

METHOD

To make oxymel

1. Put your chopped rhubarb and elderflowers into a 1 litre wide-mouthed glass jar and cover with apple cider vinegar.
2. Seal the jar and leave it to sit at room temperature away from direct light for at least one week, preferably two, shaking the jar once or twice each day to ensure the fruit is covered by the vinegar.
3. After 1-2 weeks, strain the liquid through a sieve lined with a muslin cloth. Into the liquid, stir in the honey until dissolved, adjusting the quantities according to taste.
4. When happy with the flavour, decant the oxymel into a sterile bottle, label and store in the fridge. This should keep well for up to 6 months.

To make spritzer

1. Add 2 tbsp or more of the oxymel into a glass and top up with fizzy water.

INGREDIENTS

- 2-3 sticks pink rhubarb, washed and chopped into 2cm chunks (or enough to fill your jar of choice)
- Flowers from 6-8 elderflower heads (use a fork to detach flowers from stems) or 2-3 tbsp dried elderflowers
- Raw apple cider vinegar (enough to cover the rhubarb)
- Raw runny honey or sugar (350g to every 500ml fruit vinegar)
- 350ml fizzy water

 SWAPS

Vegan: use sugar instead of honey

RECIPE BY BELINDA BLAKE

Belinda is an experienced registered nutritional therapist, lecturer and clinical supervisor at the Institute for Optimum Nutrition (ION). She is a passionate foodie and, in addition to her clinic work, runs practical hands-on workshops for children and adults interested in learning new cooking skills, trying their hand at fermentation or learning how to incorporate seasonal wild food into their meals.

 eatyourselffab.wordpress.com 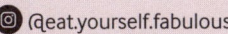 @eat.yourself.fabulous

Sponsors

SERVES	TIME	PLANTS
1	5 mins	13+

SUNSHINE SPICED OVERNIGHT OATS

"Traditional medicine has recognised the powerful health benefits of spices for thousands of years and now modern research is confirming this too. It can feel challenging to include them in our diets as regularly as we'd like, so this breakfast recipe offers a simple and delicious way to consume a variety of spices in a meal not usually associated with them. The result is a fragrant, warming and invigorating start to the day."

INGREDIENTS

- 40g jumbo oats
- 1 tbsp chia seeds
- 1 tbsp ground flaxseed
- 1 serving unflavoured whey protein or collagen
- 1 tsp cinnamon
- ½ tsp turmeric
- ½ tsp dried ginger
- 1 cardamom pod (seeds only)
- ½ tbsp raisins
- 100g Greek yoghurt
- 75ml milk of choice

Toppings

- 1 tbsp almond butter
- Chopped nuts and seeds
- Cacao nibs
- Blueberries or berries of choice

METHOD

1. Combine all ingredients except the toppings in a container and mix well.
2. Add the toppings, cover with a lid, then leave in the fridge overnight to enjoy the next morning.

⇄ SWAPS

Vegan and dairy-free: use dairy-free yoghurt and milk, and vegan protein powder
Nut-free: swap nuts and nut butter for seeds, seed butters or tahini
Gluten-free: use gluten-free oats

COLLAGEN AND CARROT CAKE OVERNIGHT OATS

CYTOPLAN

"This recipe is a celebration of simple, nourishing ingredients that come together to create a breakfast that's both comforting and invigorating. We've chosen gluten-free oats as a wholesome base, enriched with the natural sweetness of grated carrot and the warming spices of cinnamon and ginger. Each element has been thoughtfully selected, from the satisfying crunch of walnuts to the juicy burst of raisins.

"What makes this dish truly special are the added benefits of Marine Collagen and Superfood Multi, which elevate it from a regular breakfast to one that supports your skin health and overall wellbeing. It's a breakfast that's easy to prepare ahead, making it perfect for those busy mornings when you need something both nutritious and delicious. Simple, nourishing, and full of flavour — this is a dish that takes care of you, one bite at a time."

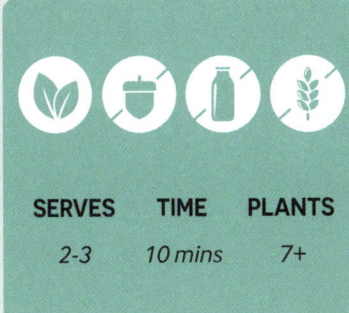

SERVES	TIME	PLANTS
2-3	10 mins	7+

INGREDIENTS

- 200g oats
- 1 large carrot, grated
- 400ml milk (or plant-based alternative)
- 3 tbsp honey
- 1 tbsp chia seeds
- 1 tsp vanilla extract
- 1 tsp ground cinnamon
- 1 tsp ground ginger
- 100g raisins
- 80g chopped walnuts
- 2 tsp Cytoplan Marine Collagen (optional)
- 2 tsp Cytoplan Superfood Multi (optional, depending on taste preferences)

METHOD

1. In a bowl, combine all the ingredients and stir well to mix.
2. Cover and chill overnight (or for at least 4 hours).
3. In the morning, divide between bowls, dust with a little extra cinnamon if desired and enjoy!

⇆ SWAPS

Vegan: use dairy-free milk, swap honey for maple syrup and omit the collagen
Nut-free: omit the walnuts or use seeds instead
Dairy-free: use dairy-free milk
Gluten-free: use gluten-free oats

RECIPE BY CYTOPLAN

For over 30 years, Cytoplan has pioneered food-based supplementation, combining the power of nature with science to create formulations that work in harmony with the body. The company's Bio-effective™ supplements are trusted by over 6,000 health practitioners and are designed to support your health for a lifetime. As an independent British company, wholly owned by The Nutritional Wellbeing Foundation, Cytoplan invests in health and wellbeing projects across the UK. Every purchase helps to support these important charities.

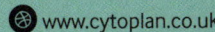 www.cytoplan.co.uk 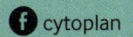 cytoplan 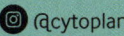 @cytoplan

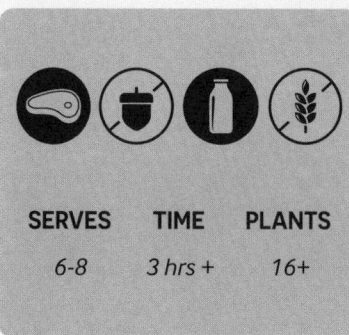
LOW-CARB CHICKEN TIKKA MASALA

"Who doesn't love a good curry? The problem is, often seed oils are used and the sauce is finished with sugar to help balance out the flavours. Here, we have used British Grass-Fed Ghee from GOOD PHATS for our fat, which not only adds flavour, but is also packed full of nutrients. It has a high smoke point, so it's perfect for this kind of cooking! We added a touch of inulin for prebiotic fibre and the perfect level of natural sweetness, without the blood sugar spikes. Serve with cauliflower rice and transport yourself to India with this recipe – metabolic health has never tasted so good!"

INGREDIENTS

- 800g boneless chicken thighs

For the marinade

- 100g natural yoghurt
- ½ lemon, juiced
- 2 garlic cloves, minced
- 1 tsp fresh ginger, minced
- ½ tsp garam masala
- ½ tsp chilli powder (we use Kashmiri)
- 1 tsp ground coriander
- 1 tsp smoked paprika
- Pinch of salt

For the masala sauce

- 1 black cardamon pod
- 5 green cardamon pods
- 2 tbsp GOOD PHATS Ghee (30g-ish)
- 1 onion, sliced
- 5 cloves
- 1 cinnamon stick
- 3 garlic cloves, minced
- 1 heaped tsp fresh ginger, minced
- 25g tomato purée
- 2 x 400g tins chopped tomatoes

Finishing the curry

- 2 tbsp GOOD PHATS Ghee (30g-ish)
- 2 garlic cloves, minced
- 1 tsp fresh ginger, minced
- 2 heaped tsp garam masala
- 1½ tsp smoked paprika
- 1 heaped tsp fenugreek leaves (curry leaves will do if you can't find fenugreek)
- 1 tsp inulin
- 150ml double cream
- Handful of chopped coriander leaves, for garnish

RECIPE PROVIDED BY GOOD PHATS

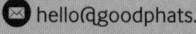 hello@goodphats.com 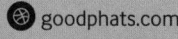 goodphats.com 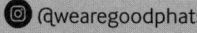 @wearegoodphats

METHOD

1. Combine the marinade ingredients in a large bowl. Cut the chicken thighs into large pieces, add them to the marinade and mix well. Cover and refrigerate for a few hours or overnight (the longer the better).

To make the masala sauce

2. Crush the black and green cardamon pods. Heat a large saucepan over medium heat and add the GOOD PHATS Ghee. Once the ghee has started to melt, add the sliced onions, cardamon, cloves and cinnamon and cook for 10-15 minutes, or until golden.
3. Once golden, add the garlic and ginger and cook for a further 2-3 minutes. Add the tomato purée and mix thoroughly before adding the tinned tomatoes. Cook this down until the tomato 'releases oil' — this should take roughly 20-30 minutes.
4. At this stage, cook further until the paste darkens considerably. Then add 300ml of water and bring to the boil. Simmer for 10 minutes and season to taste with salt.
5. Optional: for a smooth sauce, pass the sauce through a sieve into another pan, pressing down with a spoon until you are left with the spices in the sieve, and throw these away.

To finish the curry

6. Heat the ghee in a separate saucepan over low to medium heat. Add the garlic, ginger, garam masala, smoked paprika, fenugreek leaves and inulin. Cook for 1-2 minutes until fragrant, then add the sauce and double cream. Simmer gently for 10 minutes and season to taste.
7. Meanwhile, place the marinated chicken onto a tray and grill for 8-10 minutes or until charred on both sides and cooked through. Once cooked, add the chicken to the sauce along with any juices. Garnish with chopped coriander.

Serve with cauliflower rice and enjoy!

GOOD PHATS is a purpose-driven brand focused on improving the metabolic health of the world, inspired by personal health journeys and experiences of the foods we eat. GOOD PHATS offers a range of healthy fats that support metabolic health and enhance your dishes with delicious fats. From fruity Spanish Extra Virgin Olive Oil to glug over a salad, to Ghee that tastes of butterscotch to sear your steak in, they geek out on the details, as they know that not all fats are created equal.

VIRIDIAN

BUTTERBEAN AND BUTTERNUT BHUNA

"There's nothing better than a delicious, nutrient-packed, warming curry using a blend of aromatic spices including a potent organic curcumin extract. Full of natural flavour and rich in active compounds, it's the perfect recipe for any day of the week."

SERVES	TIME	PLANTS
4	35 mins	12+

INGREDIENTS

- 1 tbsp Viridian Coconut Oil
- 1 large onion, roughly chopped
- 2 green chillies, finely chopped
- 4 garlic cloves, crushed
- 2 tbsp fresh ginger, grated
- 2 tsp ground coriander
- 1 tsp garam masala
- 1 tsp Viridian Curcumin Latte
- 600g butternut squash, cubed
- 400g butterbeans (drained)
- 500g fresh tomatoes, quartered
- 2 tbsp tomato purée
- 100ml water
- 2 mixed peppers, chopped
- 100g spinach
- 20ml Viridian Black Seed Oil
- Salt and pepper to taste

METHOD

1. Heat the oil in a large pan, then fry the onion and chillies. Fry on a high heat for 3-4 minutes, then reduce to medium.
2. Stir in the garlic and ginger, then add the coriander, garam masala and curcumin powder along with the butternut squash.
3. Stir to coat everything and cook for 1 minute to allow the spices to become fragrant.
4. Add the butterbeans.
5. Blend the tomatoes and tomato purée until smooth. Add to the mix with 100ml water.
6. Simmer for 10 minutes. Add in the chopped peppers and stir well. Simmer for a further 5 minutes.
7. Add the spinach, stir through the black seed oil and add salt and pepper to taste.

Serving suggestion: serve with brown rice or green beans (for a lower calorie/carb option).

RECIPE PROVIDED BY VIRIDIAN NUTRITION

Since 1999, Viridian has been creating the purest, kindest health supplements always with a healthy attitude. The ethical formulas are crafted by expert nutritionists using clinically evidenced research to create a range of over 240 nutritional supplements, oils, tinctures and topicals. 100% active ingredients, no GMO, no palm oil and against animal testing.

Every bottle supports a charity contribution and is backed by a 100% money-back guarantee. Independently owned, Viridian sources all ingredients with 100% care so it can make a lasting difference for you and the planet.

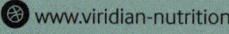 www.viridian-nutrition.com viridiannutrition 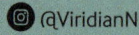 @ViridianNutrition 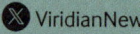 ViridianNews 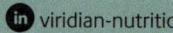 viridian-nutrition 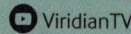 ViridianTV

ZINGY CHICKPEA CHAAT MASALA SALAD

"Salads can get very boring so add a whole bunch of spice and flavour to your next lunchtime or Indian feast with this Chaat Masala Salad. Packed full of plants, antioxidants and fibre, this will help you upgrade your brain any time of day. This is hearty enough to be a stand-alone main, or add some baked fish or hard boiled eggs. Store in the fridge for an easy lunch or snack."

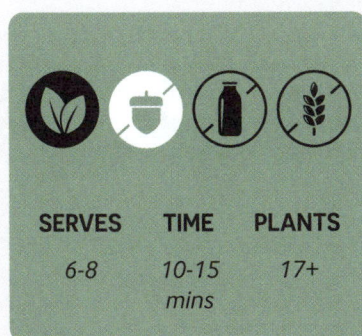

FOOD FOR THE BRAIN FOUNDATION

INGREDIENTS

- 2 x 400g tins chickpeas, drained and rinsed
- 2 medium ripe avocado, diced
- 1 medium cucumber, diced
- 2 medium tomatoes, deseeded and diced
- 1 medium carrot, finely grated
- 1 red onion, finely chopped
- Handful of fresh coriander, chopped
- Small handful of fresh mint, chopped
- 2 tbsp flaxseed, ground
- 2 tbsp chia seeds
- 60g walnuts, roughly chopped
- Juice of 2 lemons
- 1 tsp ground cumin
- 1 tsp ground coriander
- ½ tsp red chili powder (adjust to taste)
- ½ tsp black salt (or regular salt)
- 1 tsp chaat masala (or garam masala)
- 4 tbsp pomegranate seeds

METHOD

1. In a large bowl, combine the chickpeas, diced avocados, cucumber, tomatoes, carrot, red onion, fresh coriander and mint.
2. Add the flaxseed, chia seeds and chopped walnuts to the bowl. These ingredients are rich in omega-3 fatty acids and add a nice crunch to the salad.
3. In a small bowl, whisk together the lemon juice, cumin, ground coriander, red chili powder, black salt and chaat masala. Adjust the seasonings to your taste.
4. Pour the dressing over the salad and toss gently until everything is well coated.
5. Let the salad sit for about 10-15 minutes before serving, allowing the flavours to meld together.
6. Serve the salad in bowls, garnished with pomegranate seeds for a burst of colour and additional antioxidants.

SERVES	TIME	PLANTS
6-8	10-15 mins	17+

⇄ SWAPS

Nut-free: omit the walnuts

RECIPE BY FOOD FOR THE BRAIN

Founded by Patrick Holford, Food for the Brain is an education and research charity. Its mission is to create a future where the importance of nutrition in optimising mental well-being and brain health is understood by all and implemented by many. The charity provides education and resources to help people of all ages upgrade their brains. Whether it's preventing Alzheimer's and dementia, or optimising children's brains and development, its COGNITION programmes are here to create change. The charity's research is citizen science in action – doing vital independent research into how to optimise brain health through online programmes and international at home blood testing.

 foodforthebrain.org foodforthebrainfoundation @foodforthebrainfoundation

GLOSSARY

Anthocyanins: a class of flavonoids found in red, blue and purple plants, which exhibit antioxidant properties. Associated with various health benefits.

Antioxidants: protective substances that reduce inflammation and oxidative stress in the body by neutralising free radicals (byproducts of chemical reactions that can cause damage); associated with various health benefits.

Autoimmunity: the immune system's response against the body's own cells; for instance, rheumatoid arthritis and psoriasis are autoimmune conditions.

Bioavailability: the ability of a substance to be digested and absorbed by the body.

Blood sugar: glucose in the blood, levels of which fluctuate throughout the day as we eat food, and which is removed by the hormone insulin to be used in the body as energy.

Carnivore: a dietary pattern consisting of predominantly or exclusively of animal foods such as meat, eggs, fish and full-fat dairy.

Coeliac: a person with an autoimmune disease in which the body's immune system reacts to the presence of gluten in the diet, which can lead to damage to the gastrointestinal lining, malabsorption of some nutrients and fatigue.

Curcumin: a compound responsible for the yellow pigment in turmeric, which is associated with a range of health benefits, including antioxidant and anti-inflammatory activity.

Detoxification: the biotransformation and removal of naturally occurring and environmental toxic substances from the body, carried out by the liver, kidneys, intestines, etc.

Fermentation: a metabolic process where microorganisms in a food convert glucose (sugar) into gases, alcohols or acids so the food lasts longer, is easier to digest and may take on different health properties.

Fibre: a type of carbohydrate in plant foods (e.g. fruits, vegetables, whole grains, pulses, nuts and seeds) that cannot be completely broken-down during digestion. Dietary fibre supports digestive health but also has wider health benefits.

Flavonoids: antioxidant plant compounds that give foods their bright colours, and various health-giving properties.

Folate: vitamin B9, important in red blood cell formation, cell growth and function, and the healthy development of a foetus during pregnancy.

Glucosinolate: a compound found in cruciferous vegetables such as broccoli, cauliflower and cabbage, which is believed to have antioxidant and anti-inflammatory properties.

Glycaemic index (GI): a measure used to determine how quickly a food increases blood sugar levels, on a scale of one to 100.

Glycaemic load (GL): a measure used to determine the impact of a food on blood sugar levels, which takes into account both the glycaemic index of a food and the amount of carbohydrate per standard serving.

Homocysteine: an amino acid produced by the body, which is broken down with the help of vitamins B12, B6 and folate. High homocysteine levels have been linked to cardiovascular disease and dementia.

Inflammation: the immune system's response to perceived irritants, usually infection or disease, which can have negative consequences if it persists long term.

Isothiocyanate: a chemical created when glucosinolates are broken down, believed by some to have protective or therapeutic effects against a range of diseases.

Ketogenic: a diet low in starchy carbohydrates and simple sugars, which switches the body from using glucose (derived from carbohydrates) to ketones (made from fats) as its primary fuel.

Lycopene: a red antioxidant pigment found in foods such as tomatoes, which is associated with a range of health benefits.

Metabolism: the chemical processes by which the body breaks down nutrients to create energy.

Microbiome: a community of microorganisms and their environment in or on the body, e.g. the gut microbiome helps break down food and absorb nutrients.

Omega-3: essential fatty acids that we must get in our diet for cell health, brain function and anti-inflammatory processes.

Pectin: a soluble fibre present in ripe fruits that can be used for setting jams and jellies.

Phytoestrogens: compounds found in plants that are similar to the human hormone oestrogen, which some believe may have hormone-regulating effects when eaten.

Phytonutrients: compounds found in plants, which are thought to be beneficial to health and lowering disease risk.

Polyphenols: a class of antioxidant compounds thought to be beneficial to health.

Prebiotic: a type of fibre in some foods that encourages the growth and health of microorganisms in the gut, present in foods such as garlic, Jerusalem artichokes and leeks.

Probiotic: a food that contains live cultures of microorganisms, which may benefit gut health due to its potential effect on the gut microbiome.

Quercetin: a yellow antioxidant compound found in many plant foods, thought to have a variety of health benefits, including antiviral properties.

Superfood: a term sometimes used to describe a food that is deemed to be particularly nutritious or beneficial to health.

INDEX

ACKNOWLEDGEMENTS

This book was edited by Catherine Morgan and deputy edited by Hatty Willmoth. Countless hours were spent testing and tasting the recipes in this book and compiling, writing and editing its contents. We are so proud of what it has become and hope you love it as much as we do.

We are grateful to Joy Skipper for photographing the recipes in this book, to Daniela Pop for designing most of its pages, and to Salman Anjum for his design work too. Thank you to Patrick Holford, Heather Rosa and Dian Shepperson Mills for providing some of the material used in the first section of this book, and to Louise Wates for proofing its pages.

Thank you, too, to Chris Mansi, CEO of ION, for giving the green light for this project to go ahead, and to ION's trustees for their work in supporting the charity and its activities. Thanks to Carolina Geana and Anne Daly for their efforts behind the scenes to ensure this book reaches your kitchens, and to Brodie Asker for creating the index.

To our sponsors The Natural Dispensary, Cytoplan, GOOD PHATS, Viridian Nutrition and Food for the Brain, thank you for making this book possible.

Finally, thank you to our 55 contributors: ION graduates who gave recipes, words, expertise and time to this project. Thank you for your support, and for all that you do to champion personalised nutrition for health and wellbeing.

SPONSORED BY: